Vagrant CookBook

A practical guide to Vagrant

Erika Heidi

Vagrant CookBook

A practical guide to Vagrant

Erika Heidi

This book is for sale at http://www.lulu.com

This version was published on 2014-09-16

ISBN 978-1-326-02015-6

This is a Leanpub book. Leanpub empowers authors and publishers with the Lean Publishing process. Lean Publishing is the act of publishing an in-progress ebook using lightweight tools and many iterations to get reader feedback, pivot until you have the right book and build traction once you do.

Contents

Foreword

You've probably heard the old saying "Jack of All Trades, Master of None."

According to Wikipedia, it's a very old saying, with the "Jack of All Trades" part dating back to the early 1600s. Originally, it was a compliment, praising someone for their diversity and handiness. Some wiseguy later added "Master of None" and changed it to the insult we know today.

Personally, that seems unfair. The world needs generalists: people who borrow from other languages, cross-pollinate between communities, reuse old tools for new purposes. True, they're often not the deepest experts in these fields. Yet they can make valuable contributions because they have so many references to draw from. Perhaps that's why there's a modern variation of the saying: "Jack of All Trades, Master of None, but often better than a Master of Any."

Likewise, this book might say "Vagrant Cookbook" on the cover but if you dig deeper, you'll find it's about an entire ecosystem of tools. To get the most out of Vagrant, you need to know about provisioners, plugins, virtualization platforms, shell commands and more. Luckily, you don't need to master any of them (though that's always nice), you just need to be effective: A Jack (or Jill) of All Trades.

If you're new to Vagrant, this book is going to teach you how to start and help you make decisions about what tools to use. If already have Vagrant experience, the sections on alternative provisioners or multiple VMs are sure to have something new for you.

Introducing Vagrant is often a first step towards DevOps. If that's the case for you, keep in mind the two virtues of "communication" and "automation". Communicating openly will expose you to new viewpoints, new concerns and new references. Automation will let your team wield powerful tools while distributing the time investment. Together, these two things will help you grow team members who are "Jacks of All Trades, Master of Some."

This book is full of great tips and tricks for using Vagrant but there's one lesson in particular I hope you take from it. In an industry known for high stress and crazy deadlines, Erika's enthusiasm is inspiring. Whether she's automating image processing or drawing cartoon elephants, her approach can only be described as joyful.

That she channeled this energy and talent into an (excellent) book about virtual machine management should remind us how amazing computers really are. Her example encourages us to always set the bar just a little bit higher: not just in the work we do, but also in the fun we have.

Thanks for picking up the Vagrant Cookbook. You're in the right place.

– Ross Tuck

Amsterdam, March 2014

Preface

I remember very clearly the first time I heard about Vagrant. It was early 2013, on my second visit to the AmsterdamPHP meetups. The talk was from my dear friend Michelle Sanver (a.k.a. Geekie), about Open Source. She was showing how easy it is to get involved and contribute to OSS projects, by simple cloning the project repository and running the mysterious command `vagrant up`.

I started using Vagrant the next day.

A few months later, and not before facing a considerable resistance from my coworkers and the lead developer (they were using remote servers for testing - FTP upload for every single change), I was able to introduce Vagrant in the company I was working for. Although that project was quite complex and creating a Puppet provision for it was slightly painful, it was a great opportunity to learn more about Vagrant and get used to the tricks and the *automate all the things* mindset.

After leaving the company and coming back to my independent projects, I started to submit some talks for PHP conferences, and naturally Vagrant was on top of my cool-subjects list. By that time, I was presented to LeanPub and found out the amazing platform they built for self-publishing - I must say that I personally love any service that promotes independent work. It's also no news that writing is a passion for me since I was little. So, connecting the dots, it was an obvious decision: I should write about my experiences with Vagrant.

This book is based on many experiments and lots of research, from a very curious and enthusiastic Vagrant user. I tried to put together everything you need to have a pleasant experience with Vagrant, in a truly practical way.

Acknowledgments

A special thanks to all the people who helped me directly or indirectly, including Mitchell Hashimoto, Vagrant's creator, not only for sharing such a great project with the developers community, but also for personally helping me to spread the word about my Vagrant usage research.

Thanks LeanPub for providing a complete self-publishing platform for independent writers, with so many nice features.

A big thanks must go to my friend Ross Tuck for writing an inspired and truthful foreword for this book.

I also would like to thank the PHP community, and specially the AmsterdamPHP user group, for the warm welcome I received since I moved from my hometown in Brazil to this amazing city, for the awesome friends I made and all support and encouragement they gave me.

And finally, I want to thank my husband, Hugo, for being incredibly supportive with my independent projects, for the faith he has in me and in my work. This book would hardly be possible without him.

Introduction

How many times did you hear the sentence *"but it works on my machine"* ? I bet you already said that too, because, well, it happens. We can't remember all the packages we already installed and all the configurations we set in our work machine, so it often takes some time to find out what went wrong when the project was shared to another co-worker, or worst, when deploying.

Also, if we need to deal with multiple projects, how to manage the dependencies and different software versions possibly needed?

If you are not familiar with Vagrant[1], this is the right moment to get acquainted to it. Vagrant provides a portable and reproducible development environment using virtual machines, all set up in the project repository - just clone, run `vagrant up` and you're done. You will never be hostage of the *"works on my machine"* statement again; the environment is exactly the same for all developers, regardless of the operating system running behind Vagrant.

Vagrant for proprietary projects

Vagrant can make your workflow way easier when you are working on a team; having the exact same testing environment for all co-workers will avoid many problems and add much more consistency to the overall project development.

Vagrant for open source projects

Vagrant enables more developers to contribute to your open source project - just clone the repository and you are ready to go. It's not only about setting up the right environment, but also automating the process of installing a database, cloning repositories, adding data fixtures and even running tests.

---

[1]http://docs.vagrantup.com/v2/

Vagrant for devops / system administrators

If you work with system administration or any kind of server management, Vagrant is the right tool for your tests. It supports the most common IT automation tools, such as Puppet, Ansible, Salt and Chef. Experiment with different setups, build your multi-server infrastructure and make sure everything works before going to production.

What to expect from this book

As a very practical guide, this book will cover Vagrant from the requirements and installation to slightly complex tasks, such as running multiple VMs and deploying "real" servers. It will walk you through the most used Vagrant provisioners - Puppet, Chef and Ansible - showing their main characteristics and a quick guide to get you started.

This book will also cover some important pro tips to create your Vagrant projects; and finally, a collection of recipes for common provisioner tasks, such as installing packages, using templates, running commands etc.

Vagrant Cookbook is updated to cover the most important new features from Vagrant 1.5. It targets beginner to intermediate users, also serving as a quick reference for provisioners (Ansible, Puppet and Chef) and how to improve your current Vagrant setups.

Assumptions

This book assumes you are a developer experienced with command line, and you know how to setup a Linux server - you need to understand the problem before you can automate the solution, right? The tools we are going to use require some programming knowledge, since they work with concepts such as variables, conditionals and loops.

This is a book about Vagrant, for people who are comfortable with programming and also system administration tasks like setting up a web server on Linux.

The examples in this book will target mostly the provisioning of PHP web servers, but just as a way to show practical real-life examples; you don't need to be a PHP developer (and you don't need to like PHP) in order to make a good use of this book.

Getting Started

This chapter covers the basics - terminology, installation and general Vagrant usage - including how to initialize your first Vagrant virtual machine.

How Vagrant Works

Vagrant manages the process of creating a virtual machine based on your definitions, and uses automation tools such as Ansible and Puppet for provisioning the machine customization - installing packages, gathering information, performing tasks, etc.

By running a simple `vagrant up`, a virtual machine will be prepared according to what was setup on the project's configuration, and in a few minutes the project shall be up and running (let's say, a web application), accessible through your local network. You can `ssh` to this virtual machine and do whatever you want, its just like a "real" one.

It is also possible to use Vagrant for deploying real VPSs on services like AWS and Digital Ocean - we'll talk about this in the "Advanced Topics" chapter.

Terminology

Before going any further, it's important to understand some of the terms and concepts used with Vagrant.

Boxes

A box is basically a bundle containing an installed operating system (and some basic stuff), for a specific *provider* (e.g. VirtualBox). Vagrant will replicate this basic image for your virtual machine. When you setup your project, you define which base box you want to use. The box will be downloaded and imported to the system when you use it for the first time.

Host and Guest

The Host machine / OS is the one who starts vagrant. The Guest machine, as you can guess, is the virtual machine started by the Host.

Providers

A provider will handle the virtualization process. VirtualBox is the default Vagrant provider, but you could also use VMWare, KVM and others. Installation of extra plugins might be required for other providers to work. VMWare, for instance, also requires registering a license key.

Plugins

A plugin can add extra functionality to Vagrant, like supporting a new Provider.

Provisioners

A provisioner will automate the setup of your server, installing packages and performing tasks in general. Using a provisioner is not mandatory, but not using it would make Vagrant worthless, since you would have to login and setup your environment manually, just as you were used to do before (and you could just use VirtualBox alone). We have many provisioners available, from the basic Shell to complex automation systems like Chef. We're going to talk about provisioners in more detail soon.

Vagrantfile

The Vagrantfile will hold your machine definitions, and it's usually placed on your application root folder. This file is written in Ruby, but it's basically a set of variable definitions, very straightforward. We'll have a chapter dedicated to the Vagrantfile and its common configuration options.

Shared / Synced Folder

It's useful to have a common space shared between the Host and the Guest machines. With a shared folder, you can still edit your files with your favorite IDE installed on the Host machine, using the Guest machine only as a test server. However, keeping the files synced has a cost to the overall performance of your environment, we will talk about this in more detail on a later chapter.

Requirements

For provisioning your machine, Vagrant will need a virtualization software, such as VirtualBox or VmWare. The default one is VirtualBox, since it's free and open source. We will be working with VirtualBox in this book. You need to have both installed to create and run Vagrant instances.

Both Vagrant and VirtualBox are available for the main Operating Systems (Linux, OSX and Windows). Some functionalities, however, might not be present by default on some systems and it might require installation of other requirements - such as the NFS sharing functionality, that requires special packages to be installed on Ubuntu but comes out of the box on OSX.

Installation

In order to get started, the first thing you need to do is install Vagrant and VirtualBox. As said before, VirtualBox is the default Vagrant provider, the one we will be using for this book.

The best way for doing so is getting the packages directly from their respective websites, since package managers will most likely have outdated versions, leading to many compatibility problems. Head to the Vagrant downloads page[2] and to the VirtualBox downloads page[3] and follow the installation instructions for your Operating System, for both packages.

---

[2]http://www.vagrantup.com/downloads.html

[3]https://www.virtualbox.org/wiki/Downloads

Getting the right VirtualBox version

It's recommended that you check the Vagrant documentation[4] to verify which version of VirtualBox is currently compatible with Vagrant.

Updating Vagrant

Vagrant always keeps backwards compatibility, so you normally won't have any problems when updating to newer versions. It's recommendded that you keep your Vagrant updated, since the updates usually bring important bugfixes and new features.

Checking if up-to-date (1.6+)

Starting from version 1.6, Vagrant comes with a handy command to check if your currently installed version is up-to-date. Run:

```
$ vagrant version
```

If you are up-to-date, you will see an output like this:

```
Installed Version: 1.6.1
Latest Version: 1.6.1

You're running an up-to-date version of Vagrant!
```

If you are not up-to-date, the command output will inform you about the newest version available for download.

Vagrant Commands

This is a quick reference on the basic Vagrant commands:

---

[4]http://docs.vagrantup.com/v2/virtualbox/index.html

command	description	common usage
up	Boots up the machine and fires provision	When the VM is not running yet
reload	Reboots the machine	When you make changes to the Vagrantfile
provision	Runs only the provisioner(s)	When you make changes in the Provisioner scripts
init	Initializes a new Vagrantfile based on specified box url	When you want to generate a Vagrantfile
halt	Turns off the machine	When you want to turn off the VM
destroy	Destroys the virtual machine	When you want to start from scratch
suspend	Suspends execution	When you want to save the machine state
resume	Resumes execution	When you want to recover a previously suspended vm
ssh	Logs in via ssh (no password is required)	When you want to make manual changes or debug
status	Shows info about the current Vagrant environment	When you want check if the VM is already running

Global Status and Control (Vagrant 1.6+)

Starting from version 1.6, Vagrant has a global *status* and *control* feature. It allows you to check which environments are currently running, and to execute Vagrant commands in a specific environment, from anywhere in your machine.

Before 1.6, it was easy to lost track of the VMs running, and we would have to access the directory from where we run Vagrant, in order to control that specific environment. Now we can do it from anywhere.

To list all Vagrant environments currently running, use:

```
$ vagrant global-status
```

If you have one or more Vagrant environments currently running, you'll see an output similar to this:

```
id        name    provider    state    directory
-------------------------------------------------------------
037588f   default virtualbox running  /projects/project1
f47c729   default virtualbox poweroff /projects/project2
```

Now, for instance, if you want to suspend one of the environments, you just need to append the **id** to the suspend command. Like this:

```
$ vagrant suspend f47c729
```

The same is valid for the other Vagrant commands - just append the *machine id* you got from the global-status command.

 Note: a **suspended** VM will be listed as "running". You can use the halt command, providing the machine ID, to turn it off and discard the saved session.

 The global status and control will only work with environments **created** with version **1.6**. If you have an existent environment (suspended or halted) that was created with previous versions, you'll need to **destroy** it and recreate, in order to use the global status and control features.

Your first Vagrant Up

Let's "up" our first Vagrant box. The first thing we need is a *Vagrantfile*. You can manually create your Vagrantfile, or you can ask Vagrant to generate a basic Vagrantfile for you, based on the box you want to use. To get started, we are going to use the auto-generated Vagrantfile. Don't worry too much about it now, as the next chapter will be dedicated to the Vagrantfile and its most common configuration options.

First, create a folder for your Vagrant tests. Access this folder from the command line and use `vagrant init` to generate a new Vagrantfile for your project:

Vagrant 1.5+

```
$ vagrant init hashicorp/precise64
```

This command will create a default Vagrantfile, defining just one option:

```
config.vm.box = "hashicorp/precise64"
```

The `config.vm.box` will define which box your virtual machine will use. For Vagrant 1.5+, this is usually an identifier for a box hosted in the **Vagrant Cloud**[5]. The Vagrant Cloud is a new feature released with Vagrant 1.5 - it provides version control and an easy way for discovering and sharing Vagrant boxes.

Vagrant < 1.5

For previous versions of Vagrant, with no support to the Vagrant Cloud, we normally have to provide also the box URL - so Vagrant knows where to download the box from. In order to init a basic Vagrantfile with the same box (Ubuntu 12.04 64bits) you will run:

---

[5]https://vagrantcloud.com

```
$ vagrant init precise64 http://files.vagrantup.com/precise64.box
```

And it will set the following parameters:

```
config.vm.box = "precise64"
config.vm.box_url = "http://files.vagrantup.com/precise64.box"
```

Running the VM

With the Vagrantfile ready to go, it's time to boot your virtual machine. From the same directory, run:

```
$ vagrant up
```

The process of importing a box is done automatically when you initialize the virtual machine. The first time you run Vagrant with a new box, it will download and import the box to your system - it might take several minutes, depending on your Internet connection. You will see an output similar to this:

```
Bringing machine 'default' up with 'virtualbox' provider...
==> default: Importing base box 'hashicorp/precise64'...
==> default: Matching MAC address for NAT networking...
==> default: Checking if box 'hashicorp/precise64' is up to date...
==> default: Setting the name of the VM: testvagrant_default_1410896\
489249_78706
==> default: Clearing any previously set network interfaces...
==> default: Preparing network interfaces based on configuration...
    default: Adapter 1: nat
==> default: Forwarding ports...
    default: 22 => 2222 (adapter 1)
==> default: Booting VM...
==> default: Waiting for machine to boot. This may take a few minute\
s...
    default: SSH address: 127.0.0.1:2222
```

```
    default: SSH username: vagrant
    default: SSH auth method: private key
==> default: Machine booted and ready!
==> default: Checking for guest additions in VM...
    default: The guest additions on this VM do not match the install\
ed version of
    default: VirtualBox! In most cases this is fine, but in rare cas\
es it can
    default: prevent things such as shared folders from working prop\
erly. If you see
    default: shared folder errors, please make sure the guest additi\
ons within the
    default: virtual machine match the version of VirtualBox you hav\
e installed on
    default: your host and reload your VM.
    default:
    default: Guest Additions Version: 4.2.0
    default: VirtualBox Version: 4.3
==> default: Mounting shared folders...
    default: /vagrant => /media/export/Projects/vagrantcookbook/test\
vagrant
```

Ta-Da! Your first Vagrant machine is up and running. Now, log in by running:

```
$ vagrant ssh
```

You will see that it's just like a normal Ubuntu machine, connected to the Internet (as long as your Host machine is connected too), everything functional. If you run a `ls /vagrant`, you will notice that, by default, the current project folder (the root folder which contains the Vagrantfile) is shared between Host and Guest machines, so any file or directory you place inside your testing folder will be available at `/vagrant` inside the Guest.

In the next chapter, we'll see how to customize the Vagrantfile options and how to start defining automated tasks that will run right after the machine is booted through Vagrant.

The Vagrantfile

As we saw in the previous chapter, the Vagrantfile is where you define your machine settings and how the provisioning will happen. It's usually placed on the root folder of your project, under the obvious name "Vagrantfile".

The language used is Ruby, but previous knowledge on this language is not necessary, since the file is a very simple and straightforward collection of variable definitions.

Basic Example

Below, an example of a basic Vagrantfile:

```
1   Vagrant.configure("2") do |config|
2
3     config.vm.box = "hashicorp/precise64"
4
5     config.vm.synced_folder "./", "/vagrant"
6     config.vm.provision "shell", inline: "echo hello"
7
8   end
```

The above Vagrantfile will create a virtual machine based on Ubuntu 12.04 64 bits, where the location "/vagrant" will be synced with the current application folder ("./"). After booting the machine with these settings, a shell provisioner will run the inline script "echo hello" .

All this process will be managed by Vagrant when you issue a `vagrant up`.

Vagrant configuration versions

In order to keep backwards compatibility, Vagrant works with different configuration versions[6], and we must declare which version we are going to use (in the above example, the number **2** inside the `Vagrant.configure()` portion means we are going to use configuration **version 2**).

We will be using the version **2** for all examples in this book, because it's the most recent one (since Vagrant 1.1). Each version has specific configuration options, so be aware that you might run into errors if you use *version 2* options inside a *version 1* block and vice-versa.

Now let's have a deeper look into the options we can use to set up our virtual machine in the Vagrantfile.

Defining the Box

The **box** is the only mandatory option in a Vagrantfile - you must define from which base box your virtual machine will replicate. Vagrant **1.5** comes with a new way for sharing and discovering boxes - the Vagrant Cloud[7]. Now you can easily find boxes shared by the community, and you can also create and share your own custom boxes. These new boxes have version control, and they are identified by a string like **organization/boxname**.

 ### Vagrant Cloud

The Vagrant Cloud is only available for Vagrant 1.5+, and its usage is completely optional; you can keep using the "old way" (as for 1.4 and previous versions) for defining your boxes, providing a direct URL for the box file.

The option `config.vm.name` is used to define the box, like below:

---

[6]http://docs.vagrantup.com/v2/vagrantfile/version.html
[7]https://vagrantcloud.com

```
config.vm.box = "hashicorp/precise64"
```

If your Vagrant version is 1.4 or lower, the `config.vm.box` option will only define a local identifier for the box - you will also need to provide a URL or local path to the box file, so Vagrant can find and download the box to your system. This is how the same box definition looks like on Vagrant < 1.5 :

```
config.vm.box = "precise64"
config.vm.box_url = "http://files.vagrantup.com/precise64.box"
```

As Vagrant always keeps backwards compatibility, and the Vagrant Cloud usage is totally optional, you can keep using this method for defining your boxes on 1.5+ versions. The good thing about using this method is that you keep compatibility in your Vagrant project for colleagues who didn't update yet to the newest version. The downside is that you won't be able to benefit from the versioning control and unified box identifier provided by the Vagrant Cloud. It's up to you.

Finding Boxes

For Vagrant 1.5+, you can find many boxes shared by the community, and also "official" ones (from Hashicorp - the company responsible for Vagrant) in the Vagrant Cloud[8]. If you use Vagrant 1.4 or lower, you can check the website vagrantbox.es[9].

Defining a Provisioner

The option `config.vm.provision` is used to define one or more provisioners in the Vagrantfile. Below is an example that defines a basic shell provisioner usage:

```
config.vm.provision "shell", inline: "echo hello"
```

The next chapter will be dedicated to the provisioners.

---

[8]https://vagrantcloud.com/discover/featured
[9]http://www.vagrantbox.es/

Showing a post-up message (1.6+)

Version 1.6 came with a simple but yet very useful new feature. Now you can set a post-up message that will be printed every time you do a `vagrant up`. This is perfect for giving the final user some instructions about how to run or access the application / environment you just provisioned. For instance, giving the IP address where the application can be reached through the browser - like in the following example:

```
config.vm.post_up_message = "The App is up and running at http://192\
.168.33.101."
```

When you run `vagrant up` and the whole process is finished, you'll see now this message:

```
==> default: Machine 'default' has a post `vagrant up` message.
==> default: This is a message from the creator of the Vagrantfile,
==> default: and not from Vagrant itself:
==> default:
==> default: The App is up and running at http://192.168.33.101.
```

Setting up the Network

By default, Vagrant creates a NAT[10] masqueraded network between the Host and the Guest machines. Although you have access to the Internet from inside the VM, this network isn't reachable from outside, which means that you won't be able to access the application running on the Guest machine from your browser (in the Host machine).

In most cases, the private network is the way to go, because then you will be able to test the application also with other devices in the same private network, without exposing your VM to the Internet. Also, this option is **required** if you're using VirtualBox and want to use *NFS* (see the section "Setting up synchronized folders"). In order to setup a private network with a static IP address, you should add a line like this to your Vagrantfile:

---

[10]http://en.wikipedia.org/wiki/Network_address_translation

```
config.vm.network :private_network, ip: "192.168.33.101"
```

This will create a new interface on the Virtual Machine using the specified IP address. If you want to make the virtual machine accessible from other devices in your network, you need to use your current private network range.

You can also forward ports in order to expose the VM network. The following line will redirect all requests from the host on port 8080 to the port 80 in the Guest machine:

```
config.vm.network "forwarded_port", guest: 80, host: 8080
```

In this way you can point your browser to localhost:8080 and all requests will be forwarded to port 80 (normally the web server) in the Guest. However, if you run multiple VMs with the same settings, you will easily get into port collisions and this will make Vagrant throw an error.

Other options are available, but they usually are tied to a specific provider, while the above options are part of the high-level network implementation of Vagrant. To know more about networks on Vagrant, check the official documentation[11].

Setting up synchronized folders

The shared folders are essential for a good development process, since you can still edit the application files in your Host machine, using your favorite IDE, while using the VM only for running the application.

The `config.vm.synced_folder` is used to define a synchronized folder:

```
config.vm.synced_folder "./", "/vagrant"
```

The first parameter specifies which folder in the **Host** machine will be synced, and the second parameter says where this folder will be available on the **Guest** machine. By default, Vagrant already shares the current folder in the location **/vagrant** on the Guest.

---

[11]http://docs.vagrantup.com/v2/networking/index.html

If you don't specify a **type**, Vagrant will use the default synchronization functionality from the provider in use - in our case VirtualBox, and the VirtualBox shared folders. But we can improve the performance of our synced folders by using NFS, RSync or SMB.

NFS

Using NFS[12] can help increasing the synced folders performance. Vagrant (all recent versions) comes with a built-in feature that orchestrates the NFS configuration between Host and Guest.

Limitations

NFS does not work on Windows hosts - Vagrant will just ignore the request for enabling it.

Usage

In order to enable NFS, you'll add a *type* definition to your `config.vm.synced_folder`:

```
config.vm.synced_folder ".", "/vagrant", type: "nfs"
```

Requirements

NFSD: NFS requires **nfsd** to be installed in the host. This is available by default on OSX, but on Ubuntu, for instance, you will need to install the packages `nfs-kernel` and `nfs-common`.

Private Network: If you use VirtualBox (which is the most common case) you need to use the **private network** with a **static IP address** in order to use NFS - it's a limitation from the built-in network on VirtualBox.

---

[12]http://en.wikipedia.org/wiki/Network_File_System_%28protocol%29

Root Privilege: Vagrant needs to modify some system files on the host, in order to configure NFS. That's why at some point of `vagrant up` you may be prompted to provide administrative credentials (usually via **sudo**).

RSync (Vagrant 1.5+)

Vagrant 1.5 comes with a new option for the shared folders - **rsync**[13]. RSync is specially useful in situations where you can't use NFS (e.g. not supported by your Host, or not present on the Guest machine), or if you're having problems with the NFS performance.

Limitations

Unlike the default shared folders and the NFS shared folders, which keep track of all directory changes in real time, the `rsync` option is a *one-time, one-way* sharing, from the Host to the Guest machine.

If you want to work in a similar fashion as the other shared folder types, with automatic synchronization, you can use the command:

```
$ vagrant rsync-auto
```

This command will keep running until an exit signal is received (best to run it on a separated terminal). It will automatically initiate an `rsync` transfer when changes are detected in the tracked directories.

However, keep in mind that the changes inside the VM won't be reflected at all in the Host machine - on the contrary - they may be lost in the next synchronization process. Commands that generate new files in the application folder (like `composer install`) should be executed from the Host machine, in this way the changes will be reflected inside the VM when syncing.

---

[13]http://en.wikipedia.org/wiki/Rsync

Handling machine state

The `rsync-auto` command must be started only after the virtual machine is booted. It is also recommended that you stop it before turning the machine off, and when making changes to the Vagrantfile - otherwise you might experience some strange behavior. For more information about the `rsync-auto` command, check the official documentation[14].

You can also run the synchronization manually, with:

```
$ vagrant rsync
```

And the shared folders will be synchronized.

Usage

In the Vagrantfile, you will also add a *type* option to the `synced_folder` settings, specifying the `rsync` usage:

```
config.vm.synced_folder "./app",
    "/vagrant", type: "rsync", rsync__exclude: ".git/"
```

The `rsync` synced folder type allows us to exclude some directories from the folder sharing. It's recommended to exclude revision control directories such as ".git". By default, Vagrant excludes the ".vagrant" directory.

Requirements

In order to use RSync, the Host machine must have **rsync** installed (on Windows, you can use the `rsync` installed with Cygwin or MinGW).

SMB (Vagrant 1.5+)

The SMB[15] shared folders are a good alternative for Windows users, and also a new feature from Vagrant 1.5. SMB is built-in on Windows systems and can provide a better performance than the default VirtualBox shared folders.

---

[14]http://docs.vagrantup.com/v2/cli/rsync-auto.html
[15]http://en.wikipedia.org/wiki/Server_Message_Block

Limitations

The SMB shared folders are currently only available for Windows Hosts. Also, for now you'll have to clean up unused SMB folders manually, because this feature still need some fine-tuning and at this moment Vagrant doesn't remove the folders once created.

In order to delete unused SMB folders, first list them with: `net share` and then remove the ones you don't want anymore, using `net share NAME /delete` (command prompt).

Usage

In order to enable SMB, you can simply add the *type* option to your `config.vm.synced_folder` directive:

```
config.vm.synced_folder ".", "/vagrant", type: "smb"
```

Requirements

The command prompt executing Vagrant must have administrative privileges.

VBoxManage Customizations

VirtualBox has a command-line utility for making customizations to the virtual machine, like changing how much RAM memory will be allocated for it. This tool is called VBoxManage[16], and we can use it by adding some settings to our Vagrantfile.

The example below shows how to set the machine memory to 1GB:

```
config.vm.provider :virtualbox do |v|
  v.customize ["modifyvm", :id, "--memory", 1024]
end
```

---

[16]http://www.virtualbox.org/manual/ch08.html

The `v.customize` parameter receives an array with 4 items:

- **"modifyvm"** - (string) the VBoxManage command
- **:id** - this will be replaced by the VirtualBox machine ID, automatically set by Vagrant
- **"–memory"** - (string) the argument for the VBoxManage command
- **1024** - (string) a value for the previous argument

Any of the VBoxManage commands can be used in a similar fashion; you can group multiple **v.customize** directives and they will be executed in the order you define them, right before the machine is booted.

Quick Reference - Common Options

option	usage examples
config.vm.box	`config.vm.box = "hashicorp/precise64"`
	`config.vm.box = "precise64"`
config.vm.box_url	`config.vm.box_url = "http://files.vagrantup.com/precise64.box"`
config.vm.provision	`config.vm.provision "shell", inline: "echo hello"`
config.vm.network	`config.vm.network :private_network, ip: "192.168.33.101"`
	`config.vm.network "forwarded_port", guest: 80, host: 8080`
config.vm.synced_folder	`config.vm.synced_folder ".", "/vagrant"`
	`config.vm.synced_folder ".", "/vagrant", type: "nfs"`

option	usage examples
	``
config.vm.synced_folder "./application",
"/vagrant",
type: "rsync",rsync__exclude: ".git/"
```

```
config.vm.synced_folder ".", "/vagrant", type:
"smb"
``` |
```

Provisioners

This chapter will cover the main aspects behind provisioners, how they work and how to get started by using the basic Shell provisioner.

Overview

Provisioners represent the core of any Vagrant project, because without them you would merely have a fresh system to be manually setup. Vagrant supports powerful automation tools, like Puppet, Ansible, Salt and Chef. For simple tasks, you might as well use the basic Shell provisioner. The provisioners can also be used together - its quite common to have the shell provisioner along with an automation tool, for instance, for setting some environment variables or performing simple tasks before a more complex provision starts.

Shell x Automation Tools

In fact, all provisioners will execute shell commands to setup your machine, but the automation tools - Ansible, Puppet and such - offer much more power. It's like using a framework instead of writing your own *thing*. If you go for the latter, you will have to write much more code, and it can get to a level of complexity that is very hard to maintain and escalate. Using a framework, on the other hand, will require some learning time, but you will be more productive and your code will be more maintainable.

I personally consider the following features specially significant, when comparing the automation tools with the Shell provisioner:

State Handling

The automation tools have a really nice *state handling* schema, a smart way of visualizing the system through resources with a state. They will only execute tasks that weren't executed before, and they will always give you the same result (the same system state) in the end - an idempotent behavior - according to what you setup in your provisioning scripts.

Templates

Templates are very useful for setting up configuration files, for instance. Just as what you would expect from a template, they can have placeholders (variables) for dynamic content, making your provision more powerful and flexible. They usually also accept conditionals and other advanced programming features.

Open Source Modules

All the modern automation tools have an architecture that enables reuse through separated portions of code, which we'll call "Modules" for simple generalization. Tools like Ansible, Puppet and Chef provide many ready-to-use modules, either built-in or through the community of users. This can really speed up the process of creating a new Vagrant project.

Getting Started with the Shell Provisioner

The Shell provisioner is very simple, a good way to get started and understand how provisioners work, before trying one of the automation tools that we are going to discuss soon.

We can use the Shell provisioner in two different ways: *inline*, where you place the script content inside the Vagrantfile, and as a separated script file. The *inline* option is good for simple commands and tiny portions of shell script. If your script is more complex and bigger, it's better to use a separated script file.

The Vagrantfile

The first thing we need to do when setting up any provisioner is to define the *provisioner options* inside our Vagrantfile. This is done by using the `config.vm.provision` method call.

Below is an example of a simple Vagrantfile using the Shell provisioner:

```
1  Vagrant.configure("2") do |config|
2
3      config.vm.box = "hashicorp/precise64"
4
5      config.vm.network :private_network, ip: "192.168.33.101"
6
7      config.vm.provision "shell", inline: "ls -la /vagrant"
8
9  end
```

The above example uses the *inline* option; it will run ls -la on /vagrant (inside the Guest machine) and you should see the command output from your terminal running Vagrant.

In order to use a shell script file, we would just change the `config.vm.provision` line to:

```
1  config.vm.provision "shell", path: "script.sh"
```

Where `script.sh` can be a relative or absolute path, or even a URL pointing to a remote script.

Running the Provisioner

By default, a Provisioner only runs once - right when you create your environment (first vagrant up since the last destroy). This saves a lot of time in a daily basis, when you normally will be reusing a VM previously provisioned. But you can also force the execution of the Provisioner, even when the machine is already turned on.

If the environment is not yet created, you just need to run `vagrant up`. If the environment was already provisioned before, and the machine is turned down, you need to use `vagrant up --provision` in order to force the provisioner execution. And, finally, if the machine is already turned on, you will use either `vagrant provision` (run only the provisioners) or `vagrant reload --provision`. The latter will reboot the machine before running the provisioners.

Always run the provisioner (1.6+)

Starting with version 1.6, you can configure a provisioner to run every time you execute `vagrant up` or `vagrant reload`. You just need to add the option `run: "always"`, like in the example below:

```
1  Vagrant.configure("2") do |config|
2    config.vm.provision "shell", run: "always" do |s|
3      s.inline = "echo hello"
4    end
5  end
```

Automation Tools

Automation tools are, in a nutshell, powerful frameworks for server management and deploy. Since Vagrant environments are meant for development and are normally very specialized, commonly with a single node, the general usage of this tools as Vagrant provisioners is way simpler than what you would expect by reading their documentations.

In the next chapters, we are going to have a deeper look at three different automation tools supported by Vagrant: **Ansible**, **Puppet** and **Chef**. They are the three most used Vagrant provisioners, according to a usage research[17] performed in January 2014.

We will examine each tool by discussing its main characteristics, so you have a good base for comparison between them; a quick guide will introduce you to the provisioner language and conventions, and finishing each chapter you will have a practical example of a web server provision with that tool. All examples will target the exact same result - a web server running Ubuntu with Nginx and PHP.

It's important to understand that these automation tools have a level of complexity that we cannot totally cover in this book; we focused on showing their practical usage as Vagrant provisioners. The quick guide will drive you through the basics so you can understand the practical examples and experiment with different provisions.

---

[17]http://www.erikaheidi.com/2014/01/24/vagrant-usage-research/

Practical Example

As mentioned before, each provisioner chapter will have a practical example that creates exactly the same environment. We are not going to use any third party module. This will give you a better comparison between the provisioners.

The Goal

- Ubuntu 12.04, base box provided by Vagrant
- Nginx+PHP5-FPM (PHP5.5+) properly set up, accessible through the VM IP address
- **No** third party modules

The Tasks

Let's break our requirements into tasks, or steps, as if we were going to execute everything by hand.

It's not just about installing some packages; to get the newer PHP version we'll need to add a PPA (private package archiver) repository first - it's the easiest way. And we'll also need to change Nginx's default virtualhost to use PHP5-FPM.

Following, the tasks we would perform manually to get such environment:

- Run apt-get update
- Add a PPA repository to install newest version of PHP
  - Install the package *python-software-properties*, in order to use *add-apt-repository*
  - Add the PHP5.5 PPA repository
  - Run apt-get update
- Install Nginx
- Install PHP5-FPM
- Install extra packages (vim, curl, git etc)
- Install PHP packages (php5-curl, php5-cli etc)

- Setup the default Nginx website, by replacing the configuration file on **/etc/nginx/sites-available/default** .
- Restart Nginx

 Follow up the examples

All the examples used in the next chapters are available on GitHub, in the repository erikaheidi/vagrantcookbook[18].

---

[18]https://github.com/erikaheidi/vagrantcookbook

Ansible

Overview

Ansible[19] is an IT automation tool that, as many others, is capable of orchestrating tasks such as installing packages and configuring systems in multiple machines, but with one big differential: it was built with simplicity in mind. It uses YAML for its configuration files, making it totally human-readable so anyone can easily understand what's going on and learn how to create a complex provision really fast.

Ansible is probably the most straightforward provisioner available nowadays for Vagrant. Its simplicity doesn't make it less powerful; with a large collection of built-in modules, Ansible provides many advanced features with a minimalistic language.

Characteristics

Language Complexity

Ansible uses YAML and the Jinja2 templating system for its provision scripts, very simple and straightforward. The general learning curve for Ansible is low.

Execution Order

The tasks are executed in the exact order you define them.

Resources / Community

Ansible is getting more popular because of its simplicity. According to my usage research, Ansible is the third most used Vagrant provisioner.

---

[19]http://www.ansibleworks.com/

Organization / Modularity

Ansible has plenty of built-in modules, and you can write your own modules too. Tasks can be grouped into separated files and included in the *playbook*, so you can easily reuse them. The recommended way to organize a collection of related tasks and files is through the use of *Roles*.

Requirements

In order to use Ansible as provisioner, you'll need to install it in the **Host** machine.

As with many other packages including Vagrant and VirtualBox, package managers like *apt* will most probably have outdated versions, which can lead you to all sorts of compatibility problems. The best thing to do is consult the installation instructions[20] on the official Ansible documentation - it will guide you on how to install the most recent version of Ansible in your operating system.

 Windows Hosts

Windows is not officially supported by Ansible to be used as control machine (Host), but there are some workarounds. You can use **Cygwin**[21] to install all dependencies and Ansible, or you can use a Shell Provisioner[22] to run Ansible in the Guest machine, using a local SSH connection to run the tasks.

Terminology

The Ansible scripts are called ***playbooks***.

The Vagrantfile

We need to define the Ansible provisioner in our Vagrantfile, with the `config.vm.provision` method call. This is a basic example, where we just set the location of the playbook file :

---

[20]http://www.ansibleworks.com/docs/intro_installation.html
[21]https://servercheck.in/blog/running-ansible-within-windows
[22]https://github.com/geerlingguy/JJG-Ansible-Windows

```
1   Vagrant.configure("2") do |config|
2
3       config.vm.box = "hashicorp/precise64"
4
5       config.vm.network :private_network, ip: "192.168.33.101"
6
7       config.vm.provision "ansible" do |ansible|
8           ansible.playbook = "playbook.yml"
9       end
10
11      config.vm.synced_folder "../../testapp", "/vagrant", :nfs => true
12
13  end
```

Usually you won't need more than this, but there are other options you can use to customize your Ansible provisioning, such as:

Option	Description	Example Value
ansible.inventory_path	Sets inventory path	"my_inventory"
ansible.verbose	Changes output verbosity	"vvv"
ansible.sudo	Makes Ansible run tasks with sudo by default	true

For a complete list of the Ansible provisioner options, check the Vagrant documentation[23].

Quick Ansible Guide

Tasks

Tasks are defined using YAML syntax, as shown below:

---

[23]http://docs.vagrantup.com/v2/provisioning/ansible.html

```
- name: Install Nginx
  sudo: yes
  apt: pkg=nginx
```

The above example tells Ansible to install the package nginx, using sudo. The "name" property is just an identifier, for easier debug (it shows up on the output). The "apt" item is actually a built-in Ansible module[24].

Playbook

The playbook is where we're going to define our tasks. A playbook containing the "Install Nginx" task that we just saw, plus php5-fpm installation, would look like this:

```
1  ---
2  - hosts: all
3    tasks:
4      - name: Install Nginx
5        sudo: yes
6        apt: pkg=nginx
7      - name: Install php5-fpm
8        sudo: yes
9        apt: pkg=php5-fpm
```

This Playbook tells Ansible to run the defined tasks in **all** inventory hosts. The *inventory* is a file that defines the machines Ansible will control; with Vagrant, usually you will be working with a single machine, and the inventory file is automatically generated by Vagrant, under the path .vagrant/provisioners/ansible/inventory/vagrant_-ansible_inventory (in previous Vagrant versions, this file would be created in the same level as the Vagrantfile, with the name vagrant_ansible_inventory_default).

Variables

Using variables is a good practice to make your scripts more versatile. Variables are usually defined in a special "vars" section inside the playbook:

---

[24]http://www.ansibleworks.com/docs/modules.html#apt

```
1  ---
2  - hosts: all
3    vars:
4      web_server: nginx
5    tasks:
6      - name: Install {{ web_server }}
7        sudo: yes
8        apt: pkg={{ web_server }}
```

We can also use arrays - they are specially useful to loop through the same task using different values, such as for installing multiple packages. In order to do so, we use the with_items option as following:

```
1  ---
2  - hosts: all
3    vars:
4      sys_packages: [ 'git', 'curl', 'vim' ]
5    tasks:
6      - name: Install Packages
7        sudo: yes
8        apt: pkg={{ item }}
9        with_items: sys_packages
```

The **with_items** option will run the task as a loop, where each item will be used as value for the **pkg** property.

You can also define the items as a static array:

```
 1   ---
 2   - hosts: all
 3     tasks:
 4       - name: Install Packages
 5         sudo: yes
 6         apt: pkg={{ item }}
 7         with_items:
 8           - git
 9           - curl
10           - vim
```

Working with templates

In Ansible, templates are processed using the Jinja2 templating language, through the built-in module *template*[25] .

Below is an example of a template file:

```
 1   <VirtualHost *:80>
 2       ServerAdmin webmaster@localhost
 3       DocumentRoot {{ doc_root }}
 4
 5       <Directory {{ doc_root }}>
 6           AllowOverride All
 7           Require all granted
 8       </Directory>
 9
10   </VirtualHost>
```

This is an Apache vhost template. We used a variable to define the DocumentRoot, so we can have more flexibility. The variable should be set in the playbook, on the **vars** section.

In order to apply this template, you would create a task like this:

---

[25]http://www.ansibleworks.com/docs/modules.html#id242

```
- name: Change default apache vhost
  sudo: yes
  template: src=files/apache/default.tpl dest=/etc/apache2/sites-ava\
ilable/000-default.conf
```

Organization

You can place all your tasks inside the playbook, but as best practice, you should group them into separate files. The easiest way to organize your Ansible provisioning is by including the individual task files from your main playbook:

```
tasks:
  - include: tasks/init.yml
  - include: tasks/nginxphp.yml
```

This works great for a small set of tasks, but it's not recommended as best practice for provisionings that are a bit more complex. The officially recommended way to organize related tasks and other files is through the use of *Roles*. In Ansible, roles are the equivalent to *modules* in Puppet and *cookbooks* in Chef. It basically defines a default structure for your files, in order to easily reference them from inside the task files / playbooks.

Taking the previous example, we could turn the "nginxphp" and "init" task files into roles, following this structure:

```
roles
├── init
│   └── tasks
│       └── main.yml
└── nginxphp
    ├── tasks
    │   └── main.yml
    └── templates
        └── default.tpl
```

We simply moved both task files into a separate directory, placing them in a "tasks" folder under the name "main.yml". Templates should be placed in a "templates" directory. In this way, they can be referenced directly by the name. To include the roles, we need to add them to a special section "roles" in our playbook, removing the old "tasks" part. The playbook now will look like this:

```
1  ---
2  - hosts: all
3    sudo: true
4    vars:
5      sys_packages: [ 'curl', 'vim', 'git']
6    roles:
7      - init
8      - nginxphp
```

Defining Services

Sometimes we need to restart a service in order to apply some changes, specially after modifying configuration files. Instead of executing the command manually, the automation tools usually have an easy way for notifying a service and scheduling its restart.

With Ansible, we define **handlers** to manage a service:

```
1  ---
2  - hosts: all
3    vars:
4      - doc_root: /vagrant
5    tasks:
6      - include: tasks/apache.yml
7    handlers:
8      - name: restart apache
9        service: name=apache2 state=restarted
```

And through the apache.yml task file we can notify the Apache handler for a restart:

```
- name: Change default apache vhost
  sudo: yes
  template: src=files/apache/default.tpl dest=/etc/apache2/sites-ava\
ilable/000-default.conf
  notify: restart apache
```

When using *Roles*, we can place a role-specific handler inside the role folder, this will make the handler automatically available when the role is included in a playbook. Just place the handler in a file named "main.yml" inside a "handlers" folder, in the role:

```
└── apachephp
    ├── handlers
    │   └── main.yml
    ├── tasks
    │   └── main.yml
    └── templates
        └── default.tpl
```

Provisioning a PHP Web Server

Now let's get everything together to create our provision. For Ansible and also for the other provisioner examples, we are going to put both Nginx and PHP5-FPM in the same role, in order to keep things simple. Another one will be responsible for more generic tasks, such as installing *Vim* and running `apt-get update`.

Directory Structure

We will be using roles to follow the best Ansible practices. This is how our directory strucutre looks like:

```
.
├── playbook.yml
├── roles
│   ├── init
│   │   └── tasks
│   │       └── main.yml
│   └── nginxphp
│       ├── handlers
│       │   └── main.yml
│       ├── tasks
│       │   └── main.yml
│       └── templates
│           └── default.tpl
└── Vagrantfile
```

Provision Files

We have 5 files - a playbook, two **task** files, a handler file and a template file (default.tpl).

playbook.yml

```
1  ---
2  - hosts: all
3    sudo: true
4    vars:
5      doc_root: /vagrant/web
6      server_name: "{{ ansible_eth1.ipv4.address }}"
7      sys_packages: [ 'curl', 'vim', 'git']
8      php_packages: [ 'php5-curl', 'php5-cli' ]
9    roles:
10     - init
11     - nginxphp
```

Note the **sudo** option on line 3. We are telling Ansible to run all the tasks with sudo - this will save us some time when defining the tasks, since we won't need to specify the sudo option for each one.

The **server_name** variable is a pre-defined Ansible variable, a *fact*. *Facts* are information derived from other systems, in our case they represent information about the **Guest Machine**. These variables are global, you can access them through your playbooks and through your templates.

YAML and variables

If you start a value with a variable, like we did for the server_name on line 6, you must **quote it**. This is due to the YAML syntax (the curly bracket is also used for defining dictionaries in YAML).

The `{{ ansible_eth1.ipv4.address }}` *fact* contains the IP address for the **eth1** interface. You can find a list with all Ansible *facts* in their official documentation[26].

Why eth1 instead of eth0?

Remember when we talked about networking on Vagrant? Since a private network with static ip address is required in order to use NFS, this is the most common network setup. It creates a second interface on the virtual machine that connects to our private network. Usually, this will be **eth1**.

roles/init/tasks/main.yml

```
1   ---
2   - name: Update apt
3     apt: update_cache=yes
4
5   - name: Install Sys Packages
6     apt: pkg={{ item }} state=latest
7     with_items: sys_packages
8
9   - name: Make sure python-software-properties is installed
10    apt: pkg=python-software-properties state=latest
11
12  - name: Add ppa Repository
```

[26]http://www.ansibleworks.com/docs/playbooks_variables.html#id17

```
13    apt_repository: repo='ppa:ondrej/php5'
14
15  - name: Update apt
16    apt: update_cache=yes
```

roles/nginxphp/tasks/main.yml

```
1   ---
2   - name: Install Nginx
3     apt: pkg=nginx state=latest
4
5   - name: Install php5-fpm
6     apt: pkg=php5-fpm state=latest
7
8   - name: Change default nginx site
9     template: src=files/nginx/default.tpl dest=/etc/nginx/sites-availa\
10  ble/default
11    notify: restart nginx
12
13  - name: Install PHP Packages
14    apt: pkg={{ item }} state=latest
15    with_items: php_packages
```

roles/nginxphp/handlers/main.yml

```
1   ---
2     - name: restart nginx
3       service: name=nginx state=restarted
4
5     - name: restart php5-fpm
6       service: name=php5-fpm state=restarted
```

roles/nginxphp/templates/default.tpl

```
1   server {
2       listen  80;
3
4       root {{ doc_root }};
5       index index.html index.php;
6
7       server_name {{ server_name }};
8
9       location / {
10          try_files $uri $uri/ /index.php;
11      }
12
13      error_page 404 /404.html;
14
15      error_page 500 502 503 504 /50x.html;
16          location = /50x.html {
17          root /usr/share/nginx/www;
18      }
19
20      location ~ \.php$ {
21          fastcgi_split_path_info ^(.+\.php)(/.+)$;
22          fastcgi_pass unix:/var/run/php5-fpm.sock;
23          fastcgi_index index.php;
24          fastcgi_param SCRIPT_FILENAME $document_root$fastcgi_script_\
25  name;
26          include fastcgi_params;
27      }
28  }
```

Puppet

Overview

Puppet is a robust and well-stablished IT automation tool, very popular with devOps and system administrators. Vagrant supports two different provisioners for Puppet: Puppet Apply[27], which works independently without a master server, and Puppet Agent[28], which requires a Puppet Master. We will be working exclusively with the **Puppet Apply** version, because it doesn't require a server. The directive scripts work in the same way for both versions.

Puppet was one of the first tools in this fashion, so it clearly inspired newer automation tools like Chef and Ansible. This also explains why Puppet is nowadays the most used[29] provisioner for Vagrant - with a big and strong community, it's really easy to find resources such as tutorials and open source modules on the Internet.

Characteristics

Language Complexity

Puppet uses a custom language for its scripts, based on Ruby. The good point about it is that you have something very specific and focused in "one job".

Execution Order

Puppet does **not** execute the tasks in the same order you define them. You must explicitly declare dependencies between tasks.

---

[27]http://docs.puppetlabs.com/references/3.3.1/man/apply.html
[28]http://docs.puppetlabs.com/references/3.3.1/man/agent.html
[29]http://www.erikaheidi.com/2014/01/24/vagrant-usage-research/

Resources / Community

Puppet (and more specifically, *puppet-apply*) is the most popular Vagrant provisioner nowadays. It was one of the first tools of its kind, so it has a history, and a big stablished community.

Organization / Modularity

Puppet supports modules and its quite easy to find open source modules for pretty much anything you want to install, making it easy for you to build complex provisionings.

Requirements

You don't need to install any extra package in order to use the `puppet-apply` provisioner with Vagrant.

Terminology

The Puppet scripts are called **manifests**. They can be grouped into **modules**.

The Vagrantfile

We need to define the Puppet provisioner in our Vagrantfile. This is the basic setup, assuming some default options and setting the *modules* path:

```
1  Vagrant.configure("2") do |config|
2
3      config.vm.box = "hashicorp/precise64"
4
5      config.vm.network :private_network, ip: "192.168.33.101"
6
7      config.vm.provision :puppet do |puppet|
8          puppet.module_path = "modules"
9      end
```

```
10
11      config.vm.synced_folder "../../testapp", "/vagrant", :nfs => true
12
13  end
```

This will assume a minimal directory structure with a **manifests** folder in the same level as your Vagrantfile, containing a default.pp manifest (the entry point of your provisioning), as shown below:

```
.
├── manifests
│      └── default.pp
├── modules
│      └── nginxphp
└── Vagrantfile
```

Any module shall be placed inside the **modules** folder.

Other common configuration options for the puppet-apply provisioner are:

Option	Description	Example Value
puppet.manifests_path	Sets manifests path	"my_manifests"
puppet.manifest_file	Changes main manifest file name	"main.pp"
puppet.options	Adds command-line flags to Puppet	"–verbose –debug"

To see more advanced configuration options, check the Vagrant documentation[30].

---

[30]http://docs.vagrantup.com/v2/provisioning/puppet_apply.html

Quick Puppet Guide

Resources

Puppet visualizes a system through **resources**. A *resource* can be a file (or a directory, which is treated as a file), a software package, or even a user, for instance. Below is an example of a **package resource**. We define resources like this:

```
package { 'nginx':
  ensure  => 'installed'
}
```

Resources usually have a state, in this case represented by "installed". We are defining that the package *nginx* must have the state "installed", which will cause Puppet to download and install the mentioned package.

Another example, this time a file resource:

```
file { "/root/puppet.txt":
  ensure  => 'present',
  content => "vagrant cookbook"
}
```

This example would create a file named *puppet.txt* in the */root* directory, containing the string "vagrant cookbook".

For the complete list of Puppet resource types, consult the official documentation[31].

Manifests

A Manifest has a collection of *resources* defining your tasks.

---

[31]http://docs.puppetlabs.com/references/latest/type.html

```
package { 'nginx':
  ensure  => 'installed'
}


package { 'php5-fpm':
  ensure  => 'installed'
}
```

Variables

We can define and use variables in our manifests, and we also have access to pre-defined variables containing information about the system - *facts* - that can be acessed through manifests and templates. Variables are usually strings or arrays of strings.

```
$sys_packages = [ 'curl', 'vim', 'git' ]

package { $sys_packages:
    ensure => "installed"
}
```

In the above example, you notice that we can use an array of packages instead of declaring each package resource separately.

Facts

Facts are pre-defined, global variables containing information about the system, such as: IP address (from each interface), memory, timezone, operating system, amongst others. For a complete list of Puppet *facts*, check their official documentation[32].

---

[32]http://docs.puppetlabs.com/facter/1.6/core_facts.html

Task Ordering

Puppet does not execute tasks in the same order you define them. In the manifest tasks example, for instance, there's no guarantee the nginx package will be installed before the php5-fpm one. If we want to establish a specific ordering (which is essential for some tasks) we need to explicitly declare **dependencies**.

If we want to make sure the nginx package is installed before php5-fpm, we can use a **require** on the php5-fpm resource definition:

```
package { 'nginx':
  ensure  => 'installed'
}

package { 'php5-fpm':
  ensure  => 'installed',
  require => Package['nginx']
}
```

There are other ways for dealing with the task ordering in Puppet. We could rewrite the above snippet for this:

```
package { 'nginx':
  ensure  => 'installed',
  before  => Package['php5-fpm']
}

package { 'php5-fpm':
  ensure  => 'installed'
}
```

The task ordering in Puppet is quite complex, but after some practice you start to understand how it works and how to chain the tasks efficiently. Although these two methods (*require* and *before*) are the most common options for manipulating the task ordering (and enough for our manifests), there are other methods too. Check the Puppet official documentation[33] for a more in-depth view of its task ordering.

---

[33]http://docs.puppetlabs.com/learning/ordering.html

Modules and Classes

Just as with any object-oriented programming language, classes are used in Puppet to better organize your code, grouping directives together. A Puppet module is basically a way to organize classes and files that are related to each other, so we can refer to them in our main manifest.

A class example:

```
1  class nginxphp(
2    $php_packages = ['php5-curl','php-cli']
3  ) {
4    package { ['nginx', 'php5-fpm']:
5      ensure  => 'installed'
6    }
7
8    package { $php_packages:
9      ensure  => 'installed'
10   }
11 }
```

We could use this class in our main *manifest* in the following way:

```
class { 'nginxphp':
  php_packages => ['php-pear','php5-intl']
}
```

Where the array is an optional argument, and in this case it overwrites the default values provided in the class.

Modules are a great way for organizing your manifests and make them reusable. If you prefer, you can also use open source Puppet modules from the Puppet Forge[34] or from Github[35] repositories. This can speed up your project setup, but keep in mind

---

[34]https://forge.puppetlabs.com/modules

[35]https://github.com/example42/puppet-modules

that sometimes you will need to write your own modules, for more customization / more control over your provisioning.

We are going to write our own (simple) modules, in this way you'll have a better comparison between the provisioners. The minimal structure for our `nginxphp` module would be:

```
modules/nginxphp
└── manifests
        └── init.pp
```

The *init.pp* file must have a class declaration with the same name of the module (*nginxphp*).

The module might contains other folders for holding templates and static files.

Working with Templates

Puppet Templates[36] support variables and conditionals, and this is very useful to have more flexible manifests. They are writen using the ERB[37] template syntax, which is part of the Ruby standard library.

Below, a template example:

```
1   <VirtualHost *:80>
2       ServerAdmin webmaster@localhost
3       DocumentRoot <%= @doc_root %>
4
5       <Directory <%= @doc_root %>>
6           AllowOverride All
7           Require all granted
8       </Directory>
9
10  </VirtualHost>
```

[36]http://docs.puppetlabs.com/learning/templates.html

[37]http://docs.puppetlabs.com/guides/templating.html#erb-template-syntax

This is an Apache vhost template. We used a variable to define the DocumentRoot, so we can have more flexibility. The variable should be defined in the main manifest, before including the template.

In order to apply this template, you would create a **file** resource as follows:

```
file { "/etc/apache2/sites-available/000-default.conf":
    ensure  => 'present',
    content => template("apache/vhost.conf.erb"),
    require => Package['apache2'],
}
```

Templates are placed in a templates directory inside the module, in the same level of the manifests folder. For an apache module using this template, we would have a directory structure like this:

```
modules/apache
├── manifests
│     └── init.pp
└── templates
      └── vhost.conf.erb
```

The Modules Folder

Remember we set a puppet.module_path variable in our Vagrantfile? This is the folder which will hold all your puppet modules. It can be placed anywhere in your project tree, you just need to set the correct value in the Vagrantfile.

Defining Services

By defining services, we have an easy way for schedulling a service restart - necessary when we make changes to configuration files, for instance.

In Puppet, we define a service like this:

```
service { 'apache2':
    ensure      => running,
    enable      => true,
}
```

To notify a service and schedule a restart, we just need to add the "notify" option, providing the service we defined before as parameter. Taking the Apache template example:

```
file { "/etc/apache2/sites-available/000-default.conf":
    ensure  => 'present',
    content => template("apache/vhost.conf.erb"),
    require => Package['apache2'],
    notify  => Service['apache2'],
}
```

Provisioning a PHP Web Server

Let's put it all together and get our provisioning for a PHP Web Server using Nginx + php5-fpm . In order to have our code organized but not too verbose, we are going to create one simple module called *nginxphp*, which will be responsible for setting up the web server with *nginx* and *php5-fpm*.

Directory Structure

The whole provisioning uses only 3 files (one template and two manifests), but they need to be placed into a specific directory structure.

```
.
├── manifests
│   └── default.pp
├── modules
│   └── nginxphp
│       ├── manifests
│       │   └── init.pp
│       └── templates
│           └── vhost.erb
└── Vagrantfile
```

Provision Files

Following, the two manifests we are going to use, and the template for setting up Nginx default website. The *main.pp* is the entry point of the provisioning, and the nginxphp class manifest is named *init.pp*.

puppet/manifests/default.pp

```
1   Exec { path => [ "/bin/", "/sbin/" , "/usr/bin/", "/usr/sbin/" ] }
2
3   $system_packages = ['vim', 'curl', 'git']
4   $php_packages = ['php5-cli', 'php5-curl']
5
6   # first thing must be apt-get update
7   exec { 'apt-get update':
8     command => 'apt-get update'
9   }
10
11  package { 'python-software-properties':
12    ensure  => "installed",
13    require => Exec['apt-get update']
14  }
15
16  exec { 'add-repository':
17    command => "add-apt-repository ppa:ondrej/php5 -y",
```

```
18    require => Package['python-software-properties'],
19  }
20
21  package { $system_packages:
22    ensure => "installed",
23    require => Exec['apt-get update'],
24  }
25
26  exec { 'apt-update-refresh':
27    command => 'apt-get update',
28    require => Exec['add-repository'],
29    before  => Class['nginxphp']
30  }
31
32  class { 'nginxphp':
33    server_name => $ipaddress_eth1,
34    doc_root => '/vagrant/web',
35    php_packages => $php_packages,
36  }
```

The first **Exec** is capitalized because it's in fact a reference to an existent, internal exec resource. This line customizes the bin paths so we don't need to provide full command paths in our exec resources (as in the apt-get update command).

$ipaddress_eth1

You are probably wondering where this variable came from. This is a pre-defined variable, a **fact**, containing the IP address for the eth1 network interface (as we did with Ansible).

puppet/modules/nginxphp/manifests/init.pp

```
1   class nginxphp(
2     $server_name = 'localhost',
3     $doc_root = '/vagrant',
4     $php_packages = ['php5-curl', 'php5-cli']
5   ) {
6
7     package { ['nginx', 'php5-fpm']:
8       ensure  => 'installed'
9     }
10
11    service { 'nginx':
12      ensure     => running,
13      enable     => true,
14    }
15
16    service { 'php5-fpm':
17      ensure     => running,
18      enable     => true,
19    }
20
21    file { "/etc/nginx/sites-available/default":
22      ensure  => 'present',
23      content => template("nginxphp/vhost.erb"),
24      require => Package['nginx'],
25      notify  => Service['nginx'],
26    }
27
28    package { $php_packages:
29      ensure => "installed"
30    }
31
32  }
```

puppet/modules/nginxphp/templates/nginx/vhost.erb

```
1    server {
2            listen    80;
3
4            root <%= @doc_root %>;
5            index index.html index.php;
6
7            server_name <%= @server_name %>;
8
9            location / {
10                   try_files $uri $uri/ /index.php;
11           }
12
13           error_page 404 /404.html;
14
15           error_page 500 502 503 504 /50x.html;
16           location = /50x.html {
17                   root /usr/share/nginx/www;
18           }
19
20           location ~ \.php$ {
21                   fastcgi_split_path_info ^(.+\.php)(/.+)$;
22                   fastcgi_pass unix:/var/run/php5-fpm.sock;
23                   fastcgi_index index.php;
24                   fastcgi_param SCRIPT_FILENAME $document_root$fastcgi\
25   _script_name;
26                   include fastcgi_params;
27           }
28   }
```

Chef

Overview

Chef is an IT Automation tool that was strongly influenced by Puppet, but with some important differences. The task execution order, for instance, is sequential, not requiring explicit dependency declaration as in Puppet. This was enough reason for many people to migrate from Puppet to Chef in the last years.

Vagrant supports two different Chef provisioners: **Chef Solo**, the open source version of Chef that does not require a server, and **Chef Client**, which will connect as a node in a Chef Server. We will be working with the Chef Solo provisioner, since it's open source and does not require a server. The provisioning scripts work in the same way for both versions.

Chef is a very powerful and quite complex automation tool - using (real) Ruby as main script language; it's the second most used Vagrant provisioner nowadays, and the first most used by Ruby developers.

Characteristics

Language Complexity

Chef uses Ruby for its scripts, with an extended DSL for specific resources. This gives a lot of power to Chef, but to take advantage of that you will need to get familiar with Ruby. Certainly increases the learning curve if you are new to the language.

Execution Order

Chef execute the tasks in the same order you define them. This a major difference between Chef and Puppet.

Resources / Community

Chef has a big community. It's the second most popular Vagrant provisioner, and the first for Ruby developers.

Organization / Modularity

In Chef, we organize our directive scripts into *Cookbooks*. Chef provides a large collection of cookbooks in their official website.

Requirements

You don't need to install any extra package in order to use Chef Solo with Vagrant.

Terminology

Tasks are called *Recipes*, and a collection of tasks (the equivalent of a Puppet module) is called a *Cookbook*.

The Vagrantfile

By default, Vagrant will look for *cookbooks* in a directory "cookbooks" at the same level as the Vagrantfile. In this scenario, we just need to add the cookbooks we want to run:

```
1   Vagrant.configure("2") do |config|
2
3       config.vm.box = "hashicorp/precise64"
4
5       config.vm.network :private_network, ip: "192.168.33.101"
6
7       config.vm.provision "chef_solo" do |chef|
8           chef.add_recipe "main"
9       end
10
```

```
11      config.vm.synced_folder "../../testapp", "/vagrant", :nfs => true
12
13   end
```

This will run a cookbook called "main", and our directory structure should look like this:

```
.
├── cookbooks
│   └── main
│       ├── recipes
│       │   └── default.rb
└── Vagrantfile
```

However, if you want to use a different name for your cookbooks directory, you can specify it in your Vagrantfile by adding this line inside the Chef definition block:

specifying cookbooks path

```
1  chef.cookbooks_path = "my_cookbooks"
```

Quick Chef Guide

You can use pretty much anything from Ruby inside recipes, from variables to loops and conditionals. We will not focus on the Ruby language here, since it's not our objective; let's check the important conventions and common practices for Chef cookbooks, for those who aren't Ruby developers and want a quick start for using Chef with Vagrant.

Resources

As well as in Puppet, in Chef we build our provision by declaring *resources*. Resources are defined in *Recipes*, and grouped into *Cookbooks*.

Example of a package resource definition:

```
apt_package "nginx" do
    action :install
end
```

Chef has an extensive list of resource types. The *apt_package*, as the name suggests, is used to manage packages in Debian and Ubuntu platforms.

Another example, now a file resource definition:

```
file "/root/chef.txt" do
  content "vagrant cookbook"
  action :create
end
```

This example would create a file named *chef.txt* in the */root* directory, containing the string "vagrant cookbook".

For the complete list of Chef resource types, consult the official documentation[38].

Cookbooks

Cookbooks are like Puppet modules: basically a collection of files with a common scope - recipes and templates to install and configure *nginx*, for instance. The minimal structure will have a "recipes" directory with a *default.rb* recipe inside it (like the *init.pp* file in Puppet modules) - as following:

```
cookbooks/nginxphp
├── recipes
│    └── default.rb
```

Including Cookbooks

We can include cookbooks from inside recipes - this is great to create a central entry point (a cookbook named "main" for instance, setting up variables and default definitions) and just include what we need, from more generic cookbooks (nginx, php, etc) that can be easily reused.

This is how you include a cookbook from a recipe:

---

[38]http://docs.opscode.com/resource.html

```
include_recipe 'nginxphp'
```

Variables

We can define and use variables in our cookbooks, in order to make our recipes more versatile. They are usually strings or arrays of strings, as in the example below:

```
packages = ['curl','git','vim']

packages.each do |p|
  apt_package p do
    action :install
  end
end
```

We used a Ruby *each* loop to define each package resource, by looping through the array *packages*.

Note that the *packages* variable is just a Ruby variable, with a local scope. If you want to share this data with other cookbooks or with templates, (making it global) you have to create an ***attribute***.

Attributes

Attributes store data from the *node* (in our case, the node is the VM itself). Chef generates some automatic attributes with information about the system - IP address, hostname - like the *facts* in Puppet and Ansible; you can also define your own attributes in your cookbooks, and this is very useful to share data between your recipes.

Attributes are stored in a node object (just think about it as a multi-dimensional array) that is globally available. Taking the previous example (using the *packages* variable), we could make the list of packages global by setting an attribute with that value:

```
node.default['system']['packages'] = ['curl','git','vim']
```

In order to use this attribute from a recipe, you would have something like this:

```
node['system']['packages'].each do |p|
  apt_package p do
    action :install
  end
end
```

You are probably wondering why we skipped the ".default" part when referencing the attribute. Chef has different *types* of attributes, and the type is basically a precedence definition. For instance, the *normal* type has a higher precedence than a *default* type.

When **defining** an attribute, you must choose a type. Then Chef will figure out which value it should return when you request the attribute directly - you might want to have different values with different precedences.

The **default** type has a lower precedence, and it's the recommended type to be used in a cookbook. If you want to learn more about the different attribute types and which automatic attributes are available, consult the official documentation[39].

Working with Templates

This is an Apache vhost template for Chef:

---

[39]http://docs.opscode.com/chef_overview_attributes.html

```
1   <VirtualHost *:80>
2       ServerAdmin webmaster@localhost
3       DocumentRoot <%= @doc_root %>
4
5       <Directory <%= @doc_root %>>
6           AllowOverride All
7           Require all granted
8       </Directory>
9
10  </VirtualHost>
```

As you can notice, Chef templates are exactly the same as Puppet templates (ERB, from standard Ruby). The only thing that will change is the way you make variables and attributes available inside the template. While in Puppet you have direct access to *facts* and variables defined in the manifest, in Chef you need to provide the variables by adding them in the template resource definition.

To apply the template, we would have a resource like this:

```
template "/etc/apache2/sites-available/000-default.conf" do
    source "vhost.conf.erb"
    variables({
        :doc_root => node['apache']['doc_root']
    })
    action :create
end
```

Note that we need to provide the variables that are going to be used inside the template. In this example, we are using a custom *attribute* that should be previously defined.

The template file (vhost.erb) must be placed in a specific directory structure inside your cookbook:

```
cookbooks/apache
├── recipes
│   └── default.rb
└── templates
    └── default
        └── vhost.conf.erb
```

Why a "default" folder?

It's similar to what happens with the attributes: if your cookbook is supposed to work with different operating systems, you might overwrite the defaults by having some OS-specific or host-specific templates. However, as we are working with Linux and more specifically Ubuntu, we don't need to worry about this - just stick with the *default*.

Defining Services

Just like with Puppet, in Chef we define a *Service* resource to manage services.

```
service "apache2" do
    action [ :enable, :start ]
end
```

To restart the Apache service, taking as example the previous task of applying the Apache vhost template, we would have the following resource definition:

```
template "/etc/apache2/sites-available/000-default.conf" do
    source "vhost.conf.erb"
    variables({
        :doc_root    => node['apache']['doc_root']
    })
    action :create
    notifies :restart, resources(:service => "apache2")
end
```

Provisioning a PHP Web Server

Now let's create our provision. As with the other provisioners, we'll have a **nginxphp** cookbook to install our web server, and an entry point to define common settings.

Directory Structure

```
.
├── cookbooks
│   ├── main
│   │   └── recipes
│   │       └── default.rb
│   └── nginxphp
│       ├── recipes
│       │   └── default.rb
│       └── templates
│           └── default
│               └── vhost.erb
└── Vagrantfile
```

Scripts

cookbooks/main/recipes/default.rb

```
1   node.default['system']['packages'] = ['curl','git','vim']
2
3   node.default['nginx']['server_name'] = "192.168.33.101"
4   node.default['nginx']['doc_root'] = "/vagrant/web"
5
6   node.default['php']['packages'] = ['php5-curl','php5-cli']
7
8   execute "apt-get update" do
9       command "apt-get update"
10  end
11
12  apt_package "python-software-properties" do
13      action :install
14  end
15
16  execute "add-apt-repository" do
17      command "add-apt-repository ppa:ondrej/php5"
18  end
19
20  execute "apt-get update" do
21      command "apt-get update"
22  end
23
24  node['system']['packages'].each do |p|
25      apt_package p do
26          action :install
27      end
28  end
29
30  include_recipe 'nginxphp'
```

Missing Facts

You might be wondering why we didn't use a *Fact* (or automatic attribute, as they call in Chef) for the *server_name*, as we did before with Ansible and Puppet. Turns out Chef doesn't have an automatic attribute for the **eth1** IP address, so the easiest way for setting up the template is by using a static value with the same IP address we used on the Vagrantfile.

cookbooks/nginxphp/recipes/default.rb

```
1   ["nginx", "php5-fpm"].each do |p|
2       apt_package p do
3           action :install
4       end
5   end
6
7   service "nginx" do
8       action [ :enable, :start ]
9   end
10
11  service "php5-fpm" do
12      action [ :enable, :start ]
13  end
14
15  template "/etc/nginx/sites-available/default" do
16      source "vhost.erb"
17      variables({
18          :doc_root    => node['nginx']['doc_root'],
19          :server_name => node['nginx']['server_name']
20      })
21      action :create
22      notifies :restart, resources(:service => "nginx")
23  end
24
25  node['php']['packages'].each do |p|
26      apt_package p do
27          action :install
```

```
28        end
29   end
```

cookbooks/nginxphp/templates/default/vhost.erb

```
1    server {
2          listen   80;
3
4          root <%= @doc_root %>;
5          index index.html index.php;
6
7          server_name <%= @server_name %>;
8
9          location / {
10                 try_files $uri $uri/ /index.php;
11         }
12
13         error_page 404 /404.html;
14
15         error_page 500 502 503 504 /50x.html;
16         location = /50x.html {
17                 root /usr/share/nginx/www;
18         }
19
20         location ~ \.php$ {
21                 fastcgi_split_path_info ^(.+\.php)(/.+)$;
22                 fastcgi_pass unix:/var/run/php5-fpm.sock;
23                 fastcgi_index index.php;
24                 fastcgi_param SCRIPT_FILENAME $document_root$fastcgi\
25   _script_name;
26                 include fastcgi_params;
27         }
28   }
```

Pro Tips

This chapter covers some simple Pro Tips that will help you build better Vagrant projects.

Update First!

It's very important to run an `apt-get update` before starting any package installation. This must be the first thing in your provisioning scripts! It's common to face some really annoying problems when you install packages from outdated repositories. You must remember this specially when using Puppet, because sometimes you might not even know that the packages are being installed *before* the `apt-get update` - since the task ordering is tricky with this automation tool.

NFS Performance Improvement

Using NFS will improve overall performance on synchronized folders, but it's a well-known fact that things can get really slow if you have a lot of writing operations on disk - like when using cache and / or saving logs for each request made to the application running on the VM. This is a common problem for Symfony applications, for instance - the app can be somewhere between 2 to 5 times slower when running on Vagrant, against a local server environment.

The best thing to do in such situations is to move this kind of content outside the synchronized folders, and, when possible, use shared memory - faster because it's not on disk. For Symfony applications, you can simply edit the AppKernel and overwrite two methods - **getCacheDir()** and **getLogDir()** :

app/AppKernel.php

```
1    public function getCacheDir()
2    {
3        if (in_array($this->environment, array('dev', 'test'))) {
4            return '/dev/shm/cache/' .  $this->environment;
5        }
6
7        return parent::getCacheDir();
8    }
9
10    public function getLogDir()
11    {
12        if (in_array($this->environment, array('dev', 'test'))) {
13            return '/dev/logs';
14        }
15
16        return parent::getLogDir();
17    }
```

This will overwrite the default *cache* and *logs* directory definitions, only when the environment is either **dev** or **test**. It will use */dev/shm* , a shared memory filesystem (very similar to */tmp*).

This "trick" makes the application run even a little bit faster on the VM than in your default local environment. The solution was originally published by Benjamin Eberlei in his blog[40].

 You'll need to create the sub-directories inside */dev/shm* and set the right permissions, through your provisioning scripts.

---

[40]http://www.whitewashing.de/2013/08/19/speedup_symfony2_on_vagrant_boxes.html

Permission Problems

Sometimes you can face permission problems in the synced folders, when working from the Host machine and performing commands inside the Guest machine. A simple way for fixing this is changing the web server user and group to `vagrant`, on the Guest machine.

On Ubuntu boxes, this can be easily done with a grep/sed command, for both Apache and Nginx web servers. Below you can find examples on how to do this for PHP web servers on the three provisioners we covered in this book.

Apache2+PHP

You'll need to change the Apache user and group.

Ansible

```
1   - name: Check default apache user
2     shell: grep -c 'www-data' /etc/apache2/envvars
3     register: apacheuser_check
4     ignore_errors: yes
5
6   - name: Change default apache user
7     shell: sed -i 's/www-data/vagrant/' /etc/apache2/envvars
8     when: apacheuser_check > 0
9     notify: restart apache2
```

 Ansible needs a helper task in order to perform the conditional task. We register a variable with the command output, and tell Ansible to ignore if the result is 0 (in such case, it will not execute the second task).

Puppet

```
1   exec { 'ApacheUserGroup':
2       command => "sed -i 's/www-data/vagrant/' /etc/apache2/envvars",
3       onlyif  => "grep -c 'www-data' /etc/apache2/envvars",
4       notify  => Service['apache2']
5   }
```

Chef

```
1   execute 'ApacheUserGroup' do
2       command "sed -i 's/www-data/vagrant/' /etc/apache2/envvars"
3       only_if "grep -c 'www-data' /etc/apache2/envvars",
4       notifies :restart, resources(:service => "apache2")
5   end
```

Nginx+PHP5-FPM

Usually, you'll need to change only the **php5-fpm** user and group.

Ansible

```
1   - name: Check default php5-fpm user
2     shell: grep -c 'www-data' /etc/php5/fpm/pool.d/www.conf
3     register: phpuser_check
4     ignore_errors: yes
5
6   - name: Change default php5-fpm user
7     shell: sed -i 's/www-data/vagrant/' /etc/php5/fpm/pool.d/www.conf
8     when: phpuser_check > 0
9     notify: restart php5-fpm
```

Puppet

```
1  exec { 'PHPUserGroup':
2      command => "sed -i 's/www-data/vagrant/' /etc/php5/fpm/pool.d/ww\
3  w.conf",
4      onlyif  => "grep -c 'www-data' /etc/php5/fpm/pool.d/www.conf",
5      notify  => Service['php5-fpm']
6  }
```

Chef

```
1  execute 'PHPUserGroup' do
2      command "sed -i 's/www-data/vagrant/' /etc/php5/fpm/pool.d/www.c\
3  onf"
4      only_if "grep -c 'www-data' /etc/php5/fpm/pool.d/www.conf"
5      notifies :restart, resources(:service => "php5-fpm")
6  end
```

Debugging

If you get errors during the provision process, it might be a good idea to increase the verbosity of the provisioner. We can do this by editing our Vagrantfile and adding an extra option to the provision block:

Increasing verbosity: Ansible

```
1      config.vm.provision "ansible" do |ansible|
2          ansible.playbook = "playbook.yml"
3          ansible.verbose = 'vvv' #accepted values: from 'v' to 'vvvv'
4      end
```

Increasing verbosity: Puppet

```
1    config.vm.provision :puppet do |puppet|
2        puppet.module_path = "modules"
3        puppet.options = "--verbose --debug"
4    end
```

Increasing verbosity: Chef

```
1    config.vm.provision "chef_solo" do |chef|
2        chef.add_recipe "main"
3        chef.log_level = :debug
4    end
```

Login, Fix, Automate

If the provision runs but the result is not working as expected, or when you need to setup something very specific that you are not familiar with, its a good idea to log in, explore and fix things before automating.

Build your provision step by step. Use `vagrant provision` after changing the provision scripts, this will apply only what you changed. When you feel confident that everything is working, use `vagrant destroy` to start from scratch. It will clear all the previous changes to the box, and when you run `vagrant up` again the provision will be executed from the start.

VirtualBox Guest Additions

In some cases, it might be necessary to install / update the *VirtualBox Guest Additions* - a package that enables additional features on the Guest machine. Usually, it's already present on base boxes, but as an outdated version. If you are having trouble with shared folders and NFS, it might be a good idea to do it. There's a built-in Vagrant plugin for automatically install the Guest Additions, you just need to run:

```
1  vagrant plugin install vagrant-vbguest
```

However, by default this plugin will try to auto update the Guest Additions each time you reboot the machine, which can be annoying. You can disable the auto-update, but in this case you'll need to run the update manually. For more information about this plugin usage and settings, see the vbguest plugin documentation[41].

---

[41]https://github.com/dotless-de/vagrant-vbguest

Advanced Topics

This chapter covers some advanced topics for more specific Vagrant usages.

Running Multiple Virtual Machines

With Vagrant, you can easily run multiple Virtual Machines using a single Vagrant-file. There are many use cases for this, but usually this environment is created to represent a real-life application that uses multiple servers - like separated database and web servers, for instance.

You can also use this functionality to easily benchmark different environments or to test different provisioners.

The Vagrantfile

Below is an example of a Vagrantfile setting up multiple virtual machines. This will configure a web server and a database server:

```
1  Vagrant.configure("2") do |config|
2
3      config.vm.box = "hashicorp/precise64"
4
5      config.vm.synced_folder "./", "/vagrant"
6
7      config.vm.define "web" do |web|
8
9          web.vm.network :private_network, ip: "192.168.33.101"
10
11         web.vm.provision "ansible" do |ansible|
12             ansible.playbook = "ansible/playbook_webserver.yml"
```

```
13          end
14
15          web.vm.synced_folder "./myapp/", "/vagrant", :nfs => true
16      end
17
18      config.vm.define "db" do |db|
19
20          db.vm.network :private_network, ip: "192.168.33.102"
21
22          db.vm.provision "ansible" do |ansible|
23              ansible.playbook = "ansible/playbook_dbserver.yml"
24          end
25      end
26
27  end
```

In order to define multiple VMs in the Vagrantfile, we use the `config.vm.define` method call. This block works exactly in the same way as the main `Vagrant.configure` block, while the server identifiers - **web** and **db** - are the equivalent of the **config** object in the main block. You can use the same methods (vm.network, vm.provision, vm.box etc) to define machine-specific settings.

The values inside the `config.vm.define` block will overwrite the default values that you setup with the **config** object - look at the *synced_folder* definition: there's a default value in the top of the Vagrantfile, but for the web server we overwrite it in order to serve the application files.

We used the same box for both servers, by defining it only once in the main section. If we wanted to use a different box for the database server, for instance, we would only need to overwrite the box values (vm.box, vm.box_url) inside the **db** block.

Controlling Multiple VMs

When you have a Vagrantfile with multiple Virtual Machines defined, the default behavior of Vagrant is to apply the commands to all the machines. So when you run `vagrant up`, all machines defined in the Vagrantfile will be initialized, one at a time, in the order you defined them.

To control the machines individually, you just need to add the machine identifier to the command. For instance, considering the above Vagrantfile, if we wanted to boot only the web server, we would run:

```
$ vagrant up web
```

You can even use a regular expression to turn on a group of machines. Imagine you have a group of 10 database servers, with similar names like: **data1**, **data2**, **data3** (...) **data10**.

To turn on the machines from 1 to 5, you could simply run:

```
$ vagrant up /data[1-5]/
```

Provisioning VPSs on cloud services

Vagrant has some special providers that can create "real" servers on Digital Ocean, Amazon AWS and other cloud services. The process involves installing a plugin and adding some required options to the provider block on the Vagrantfile, usually setting SSH keys and service credentials. Let's see how we can create a Digital Ocean droplet with the Ansible provision we created before.

Using the Digital Ocean Provider

First we need to install the Digital Ocean provider:

```
$ vagrant plugin install vagrant-digitalocean
```

If you don't have generated SSH keys yet, do it now - use the defaults and leave the passphrase blank.

```
$ cd ~/.ssh
$ ssh-keygen -t rsa
```

For more detailed instructions, check this link[42] (steps 1 and 2).

Now, log in to your Digital Ocean account to generate your API key. Go to the **API**[43] tab and click on the "Create" link. We're going to use both the Client ID and this API key inside our Vagrantfile.

Following, an example of a Vagrantfile using the Digital Ocean provider, and the Ansible provision we used before (Nginx+PHP5-FPM).

The box used is provided by the plugin creators, and it's special for the Digital Ocean provider. It doesn't have an operating system, as with other boxes we are used to work with. In order to choose which operating system will be used in this box, you'll have to specify an option inside the provider block, in the Vagrantfile.

You need to fill in your Digital Ocean Client ID and API Key. You can also choose which image and region you want to use when creating your droplet. In this example, we are going to use a Ubuntu 14.04 x64 droplet in the New York 2 region.

To see the complete list of configuration options and features of the Digital Ocean provider, have a look at their Github repository[44].

Vagrantfile

```
1   Vagrant.configure("2") do |config|
2
3       config.vm.box = "digital_ocean"
4       config.vm.box_url = "https://github.com/smdahlen/vagrant-digital\
5   ocean/raw/master/box/digital_ocean.box"
6
7       config.ssh.private_key_path = "~/.ssh/id_rsa"
8
9       config.vm.provider :digital_ocean do |provider|
10          provider.token = 'YOUR TOKEN'
```

---

[42]https://www.digitalocean.com/community/articles/how-to-set-up-ssh-keys--2

[43]https://cloud.digitalocean.com/api_access

[44]https://github.com/smdahlen/vagrant-digitalocean

```
11          provider.image = 'Ubuntu 14.04 x64'
12          provider.region = 'nyc2'
13          provider.size = '512mb'
14      end
15
16      config.vm.provision "ansible" do |ansible|
17          ansible.playbook = "ansible/playbook.yml"
18      end
19
20      config.vm.synced_folder "../testapp", "/vagrant"
21
22  end
```

When using a provider other than VirtualBox, you must specify it when running vagrant up. For the Digital Ocean provider, you'll use:

```
$ vagrant up --provider=digital_ocean
```

And the output produced by Vagrant will be similar to this:

```
Bringing machine 'default' up with 'digital_ocean' provider...
[default] Using existing SSH key: Vagrant
[default] Creating a new droplet...
[default] Assigned IP address: 188.226.159.108
[default] Rsyncing folder: /media/export/Projects/vagrantcookbook/te\
stapp/ => /vagrant...
[default] Running provisioner: ansible...

PLAY [all] ***************************************************************

GATHERING FACTS *********************************************************
ok: [default]

TASK: [init | Update apt] ***********************************************
```

```
ok: [default]

TASK: [init | Install Sys Packages] ****************************
changed: [default] => (item=curl,vim,git)

TASK: [init | make sure python-software-properties is installed] **
changed: [default]

TASK: [init | Add ppa Repository] ******************************
changed: [default]

TASK: [init | Update apt] *************************************
ok: [default]

TASK: [nginxphp | Install Nginx] ******************************
changed: [default]

TASK: [nginxphp | Install php5-fpm] ****************************
changed: [default]

TASK: [nginxphp | Change default nginx site] ********************
changed: [default]

TASK: [nginxphp | Install PHP Packages] ************************
changed: [default] => (item=php5-curl,php5-cli)

NOTIFIED: [restart nginx] *************************************
changed: [default]

PLAY RECAP ***********************************************
default              : ok=11   changed=8    unreachable=0    failed=0 \
```

Try this example

This functional example is available on Github[45], you just need to edit the Vagrantfile and add your Digital Ocean credentials.

Note that we don't define a network - the provider will take care of this step and output the assigned IP address you got. The synced folder will be **rsynced** to the droplet. After the droplet is successfully created, the provision will run.

If you make any changes to the provision scripts or the synced files, you can just run `vagrant provision` and, as expected for a local VM, the droplet state will be updated.

ProTip

If you notice that the droplet is being created but the provision is not working, increase the verbosity of the provisioner to check what is going on.

Ansible SSH errors

If you destroy and create the droplet multiple times, you will probably get the same IP address each time you run Vagrant. The Host verification key will change for that IP, this will make SSH throw an error and the Ansible provision won't run). In such case, you'll have to remove the stored key from your `known_hosts`.

Custom Boxes

In some cases, when you need to provision complex environments, or when you can't "afford" spending time and / or bandwidth downloading a lot of packages, building a custom box can be a good solution. You just need to keep in mind that the packages

---

[45]https://github.com/erikaheidi/vagrantcookbook/tree/master/provider_digitalocean

can get outdated easily, so you'll eventually need to update the system and rebuild the box.

The easiest way for doing so is by reusing an existent base box - you can simply customize it to your needs and *repackage* the box using Vagrant. Creating a box from the ground is also possible, but it's a slightly complex process since you have to meet some very specific requirements. Below you will find instructions on how to repackage a VirtualBox box.

Repackaging a box

Creating a box from an existent VM is quite easy. Let's first create a directory to build and save our custom box.

```
$ mkdir custombox
$ cd custombox
```

Now we need to import the base box we want to use, if it's not already present on the system. For a list of current imported boxes, run:

```
$ vagrant box list
```

If the box you want to use as base is not already imported, you'll need to import it now. For Vagrant >= 1.5, you can use any box from the Vagrant Cloud. In order to add a box from the Vagrant Cloud, run:

```
$ vagrant box add hashicorp/precise64
```

If you are using a version prior to 1.5, you'll need to provide also the box URL:

```
$ vagrant box add precise64 http://files.vagrantup.com/precise64.box
```

Now let's initialize a basic Vagrantfile for this box. This is just to make it easier for us to find out the VM name - normally Vagrant uses an auto-generated one, based on the folder name and the current timestamp. We'll need this identifier when repacking.

```
$ vagrant init precise64
```

Edit the generated Vagrantfile and add this customization:

```
config.vm.provider "virtualbox" do |v|
  v.name = "my_custom_vm"
end
```

This will setup the box name, so we can easily identify it.

 Currently active VMs

To see which VMs are currently active on VirtualBox and in which state (running, powered off, suspended), you can just open the GUI and check the list on the left. The name showed there is the name you'll need for the repack.

You can now run **vagrant up** to turn on the machine, then login with **vagrant ssh** and proceed with your customizations. When you are done with the box, you just need to run:

```
$ vagrant package --base my_custom_vm
```

This command will generate a new box file named `package.box` in the current directory. To test the new box, repeat the previous process of adding a new box:

```
$ vagrant box add custombox package.box
```

Now you can use the box **custombox** in any Vagrantfile - it will only be available in your system, naturally. If other people are supposed to use this box, you'll need to make it accessible in some way that Vagrant can download it.

Sharing boxes in the Vagrant Cloud

Public boxes can be shared for free in the Vagrant Cloud, however the free account doesn't allow the upload of boxes. In this case, you should host your .box file in some other web-accessible location, and provide the link to this file, when including the box in the Vagrant Cloud. The Vagrant Cloud[46] has some special plans that enable the upload for boxes, including private ones.

---

[46]https://vagrantcloud.com/pricing

Vagrant Share

Vagrant 1.5 came with a very useful new feature, *Vagrant Share*. It provides an easy way for sharing your Vagrant environment with people around the world. For the HTTP Share, they don't even need to have Vagrant installed in order to access your environment. This is extremely helpful for testing applications before they go live, and also for experimenting with APIs and web hooks.

In order to use the Vagrant Share functionality, you need to have an account in the Vagrant Cloud. You will be asked to log in via command line, before sharing your environment.

Logging In

The first thing you need to do in order to use Vagrant Share is to create an account at the Vagrant Cloud[47]. Once you did that, go to your Vagrant project directory and log in, by running:

```
$ vagrant login
```

Log in by providing your username or email and password. When you see the message "You're now logged in!" you are good to go ahead.

Sharing your Environment

The command `vagrant share` will connect you to the Vagrant Cloud and generate a random, temporary domain name where your virtual machine can be reached through the Internet. Direct connections are only allowed for port 80, however, as we are going to see in a few moments, you can connect with other ports in a remote virtual machine by using `vagrant connect`.

---

[47]https://vagrantcloud.com/

HTTP Share

By default, when running **vagrant share**, Vagrant will provide you with a URL that can be shared with anyone over the Internet. They don't need to have Vagrant installed in order to access the web server running in your Vagrant environment.

To run the HTTP Share, you just need to execute:

```
$ vagrant share
```

And you will see an output similar to this:

```
==> default: Detecting network information for machine...
    default: Local machine address: 192.168.33.101
    default: Local HTTP port: 80
    default: Local HTTPS port: disabled
==> default: Checking authentication and authorization...
==> default: Creating Vagrant Share session...
    default: Share will be at: sizzling-warthog-9529
==> default: Your Vagrant Share is running! Name: sizzling-warthog-9\
529
==> default: URL: http://sizzling-warthog-9529.vagrantshare.com
```

This command will keep running until you give it an exit sign. As you can see, Vagrant generates a random name for your environment. With the Vagrant Cloud in the middle, any request to port 80 of this domain will be forwarded to your virtual machine (port 80, web server).

If you access your account at the Vagrant Cloud, and go to the *Shares*[48] menu, you'll notice that all your shares are listed there, including the ones that already expired. By default, Vagrant sets an expire limit of 1 hour for each share.

 Publicly accessible

The URL provided by the HTTP share can be accessed by **anyone** who knows it. Be careful if your application shows up sensitive information.

---

[48]https://vagrantcloud.com/shares

Disabling the HTTP Share

If you want to disable this functionality of Vagrant Share, you need to provide an extra flag to the share command:

```
$ vagrant share --disable-http
```

By disabling the HTTP Share, your environment will only be accessible via **vagrant connect**.

SSH Share

The **vagrant share** command will make only port 80 publicly available for the outside; for instance, you won't be able to SSH directly to that temporary domain name Vagrant gave you. But if you use Vagrant and the Vagrant Cloud as a middleware, you can connect to any port on the remote virtual environment, by using **vagrant connect**. We are going to talk more about vagrant connect in a few moments.

The **SSH Share** is a more secure way for enabling SSH access via **vagrant connect**. When you run **vagrant share** with the SSH option, a new SSH keypair will be generated, valid only for that share (it's discarded afterwards). You can even set a limit for **one unique access** using that key.

In order to enable the SSH Share, you just need to provide a --ssh flag when running vagrant share:

```
$ vagrant share --ssh
```

And the output will be similar to this:

```
==> default: Detecting network information for machine...
    default: Local machine address: 192.168.33.101
    default: Local HTTP port: 80
    default: Local HTTPS port: disabled
    default: SSH Port: 22
==> default: Generating new SSH key...
    default: Please enter a password to encrypt the key:
    default: Repeat the password to confirm:
    default: Inserting generated SSH key into machine...
==> default: Checking authentication and authorization...
==> default: Creating Vagrant Share session...
    default: Share will be at: easy-monster-9467
==> default: Your Vagrant Share is running! Name: easy-monster-9467
==> default: URL: http://easy-monster-9467.vagrantshare.com
==> default:
==> default: You're sharing with SSH access. This means that another\
 user
==> default: simply has to run `vagrant connect --ssh easy-monster-9\
467`
==> default: to SSH to your Vagrant machine.
==> default:
==> default: Because you encrypted your SSH private key with a passw\
ord,
==> default: the other user will be prompted for this password when \
they
==> default: run `vagrant connect --ssh`. Please share this password\
 with them
==> default: in some secure way.
```

Now, for connecting to this virtual machine, the other part will run **vagrant connect** with the SSH option:

```
$ vagrant connect --ssh easy-monster-9467
```

The connecting user will then be asked to provide the password you defined for the key.

If you want to allow only one unique access, you just need to use the flag --ssh-once:

```
$ vagrant share --ssh --ssh-once
```

This will make Vagrant destroy the generated keypair right after the first connection, so no one else will be able to log in using that key.

Vagrant Connect

The **vagrant connect** command (without the --ssh option) will create a tiny virtual machine to handle the routing between you and a remote Vagrant environment, with the Vagrant Cloud in the middle. The remote virtual machine will then be accessible from a local network.

You could use this method for connecting via SSH into any virtual machine shared with **vagrant share**, even if it wasn't shared using the **--ssh** option. You'll need only the name of the share and **valid credentials**.

Let's consider someone shared a Vagrant environment with you using the default **vagrant share** command, with no further options. Now we are going to establish a connection to this virtual machine by using **vagrant connect**:

```
$ vagrant connect immense-armadillo-9764
```

The output of this command will be similar to this (the middle part was suppressed because it was not relevant):

```
==> connect: Loading share 'immense-armadillo-9764'...
==> connect: Connecting to: immense-armadillo-9764
==> connect: Starting a VM for a static connect IP. This will take a\
 few moments.
    connect: Box 'hashicorp/connect-vm' could not be found. Attempti\
ng to find and install...
    connect: Box Provider: virtualbox
    connect: Box Version: >= 0
    connect: Loading metadata for box 'hashicorp/connect-vm'
    connect: URL: https://vagrantcloud.com/hashicorp/connect-vm
    connect: Adding box 'hashicorp/connect-vm' (v0.1.0) for provider\
: virtualbox
    connect: Downloading: https://vagrantcloud.com/hashicorp/connect\
-vm/version/1/provider/virtualbox.box
    connect: Successfully added box 'hashicorp/connect-vm' (v0.1.0) \
for 'virtualbox'!

[output suppressed - box being initialized]

==> connect: Connect is running!
==> connect: SOCKS address: 127.0.0.1:33595
==> connect: Machine IP: 172.16.0.2
==> connect:
==> connect: Vagrant has successfully connected to the remote shared\
 machine!
==> connect: You can either use the machine IP above to talk to it l\
ike any other
==> connect: computer, or you can configure your software to use a s\
tandard
==> connect: SOCKS5 proxy at the address above. With either method, \
you'll be able
==> connect: to communicate with the shared machine.
==> connect:
==> connect: If you're having trouble communicating, verify that the\
 shared machine
```

```
==> connect: has given you access to the specified ports.
==> connect:
==> connect: Press Ctrl-C to stop connection.
```

As you can see from the output, Vagrant will initialize a VM using the box `hashicorp/connect-vm`. This virtual machine is very small, used only to create a routing between your local environment and a remote Vagrant environment. When the process is done, Vagrant will give you an IP address (private network) that you can use to connect directly to the remote virtual machine.

Now you can SSH directly to the provided IP address (172.16.0.2), as long as you have credentials - which leads to the next section - you **really** have to pay attention to some security concerns when using **any** share method described here.

Securing your Shares

Anytime you run **vagrant share**, you will expose your virtual environment to be accessed via **vagrant connect** - including SSH access, because all available ports will be forwarded. With the default settings present on most public boxes, it's really easy to gain access to any share, just by knowing the share name.

For now, there isn't a way for blocking `vagrant connect`, since it is the underlying mechanism that makes the HTTP and SSH shares possible. Below you will find 2 basic procedures that will make your shares more secure, avoiding unauthorized connections to your VM:

1. Change the SSH settings to disable password authentication

With the default options present on the majority of boxes, anyone who knows the name of your share will be able to connect via SSH, by using *vagrant connect* and then logging in with the username **vagrant** and password **vagrant**, which is default. To avoid this, it's **strongly** recommended that you disable *Password Authentication* in your SSH settings. On Ubuntu servers, for instance, you just need to edit the file `/etc/ssh/ssh_config` and add this option:

```
PasswordAuthentication no
```

Then restart sshd with `sudo service ssh restart`, for the changes to take effect. After that, the VM will only allow logins using key-based authentication. And if you want to enable SSH access to someone, use the **SSH Share** method, as previously described.

2. Change the default SSH keypair used by Vagrant

Public boxes usually come with an insecure SSH keypair[49] that is provided by Vagrant. Since these keys are publicly available, it's really easy to use the private key for logging in, if you don't change the keys used by your box.

In order to change the default keypair, you'll need to add a new public key to the `authorized_keys` inside the VM, and remove the existent one. You'll also need to add an option to your Vagrantfile, telling Vagrant where to find your private key - inside your Host machine.

A quick guide to perform these tasks follows:

2.1. Create a new SSH keypair

To generate a new SSH keypair, in your Host machine, run:

```
$ ssh-keygen -t rsa -C "your_email@example.com"
```

It's recommended that you leave the passphrase blank, otherwise when you run `vagrant up` you will be asked to provide the password multiple times.

2.2. Change the authorized_keys in the Guest

Now, log in with `vagrant ssh` and edit the file ~/.ssh/authorized_keys. You need to remove the current insecure public key and add your own public key there. Copy the contents of the file `id_rsa.pub` - from your Host machine - to this file inside the Guest.

---

[49]https://github.com/mitchellh/vagrant/tree/master/keys

2.3. Add the private key path to your Vagrantfile

Once you added your own key and removed the insecure one, you just need to add an option to your Vagrantfile, telling Vagrant where to find your private key (in the Host machine):

```
config.ssh.private_key_path = "~/.ssh/id_rsa"
```

 # Making the changes permanent

It's important to remember that each time you destroy the environment (e.g. with `vagrant destroy`) and recreate it from scratch, you will lose all changes, which means that both the Password Authentication and the insecure keypair will be there again. If you want a more definitive solution, you should repack the box after making these changes.

Recipes

This chapter has a collection of useful snippets of code to perform common tasks when setting up a provision, like installing packages, applying templates and running commands, on the three provisioners we saw before (Ansible, Puppet and Chef). Just a (really) quick reference guide.

System

Running a Command

Ansible

```
1   - name: Run Composer
2     shell: composer install chdir=/vagrant creates=/vagrant/vendor/aut\
3   oload.php
```

Puppet

```
1   exec { "composer-install":
2     cwd     => "/vagrant",
3     command => "composer install",
4     creates => "/vagrant/vendor/autoload.php",
5   }
```

Chef

```
1  execute "composer-install" do
2      cwd '/vagrant'
3      command "composer install"
4      creates '/vagrant/vendor/autoload.php'
5  end
```

 Creates

The creates option tells the provisioner to only run the command when that file doesn't exist yet.

Changing directory permissions

Ansible

```
1  - name: Change cache dir permission
2      file: path=/vagrant/app/cache mode=0777 owner=vagrant group=vagrant
```

Puppet

```
1    file { '/vagrant/app/cache':
2      ensure  => 'directory',
3      owner   => "vagrant",
4      group   => "vagrant",
5      mode    => 777,
6    }
```

Chef

```
1  directory "/vagrant/app/cache" do
2     owner "vagrant"
3     group "vagrant"
4     mode 0777
5     action :create
6  end
```

Creating a symlink

Ansible

```
1  - name: creating a symlink
2    file: path=/vagrant/mylink state=link src=/root/original_file
```

Puppet

```
1  file { "/vagrant/mylink":
2     ensure  => 'link',
3     target  => "/root/original_file",
4  }
```

Chef

```
1  link "/vagrant/mylink" do
2    to "/root/original_file"
3  end
```

Packages

Running apt-get update

Ansible

```
1  - name: Update apt
2      apt: update_cache=yes
```

Puppet

```
1  exec { 'apt-get update':
2      command => 'apt-get update',
3  }
```

Chef

```
1  execute "apt-get update" do
2      command "apt-get update"
3  end
```

Installing one package

Ansible

```
1  - name: Install Curl
2      sudo: yes
3      apt: pkg=curl state=latest
```

Puppet

```
1  package { 'curl':
2      ensure  => "installed",
3  }
```

Chef

```
1  apt_package "curl" do
2      action :install
3  end
```

Installing multiple packages

Ansible

```
1  - name: Install PHP Modules
2    apt: pkg={{ item }} state=latest
3    with_items:
4      - php5-curl
5      - php5-cli
6      - php5-mysql
```

Puppet

```
1  $php_packages = ['php5-cli', 'php5-curl', 'php-pear']
2
3  package { $php_packages:
4    ensure => "installed",
5  }
```

Chef

```
1  php_packages = ['php5-cli','php5-curl','php5-mysql']
2
3  php_packages.each do |p|
4      apt_package p do
5          action :install
6      end
7  end
```

Adding a PPA repository

Ansible

```
1  - name: make sure python-software-properties is installed
2    apt: pkg=python-software-properties state=latest
3
4  - name: Add ppa Repository
5    apt_repository: repo='ppa:ondrej/php5'
```

Puppet

```
1  package { 'python-software-properties':
2    ensure  => "installed",
3  }
4
5  exec { 'add-repository':
6    command => "add-apt-repository ppa:ondrej/php5 -y",
7    require => Package['python-software-properties'],
8  }
```

Chef

```
1  apt_package "python-software-properties" do
2      action :install
3  end
4
5  execute "add-apt-repository" do
6      command "add-apt-repository ppa:ondrej/php5 -y"
7  end
```

Other

Applying a Template

Ansible

```
1  - name: Change default nginx site
2    template: src=files/nginx/default.tpl dest=/etc/nginx/sites-availa\
3  ble/default
4    notify: restart nginx
```

Puppet

```
1    file { "/etc/nginx/sites-available/default":
2      ensure  => 'present',
3      content => template("nginxphp/nginx/vhost.erb"),
4      notify  => Service['nginx'],
5    }
```

Chef

```
1  template "/etc/nginx/sites-available/default" do
2      source "vhost.erb"
3      variables({
4          :doc_root    => '/vagrant',
5          :server_name => 'vagrant.test'
6      })
7      action :create
8      notifies :restart, resources(:service => "nginx")
9  end
```

Conditional Execution

Ansible

```
1  - name: Check default apache user
2    shell: grep -c 'www-data' /etc/apache2/envvars
3    register: apacheuser_check
4    ignore_errors: yes
5
6  - name: Change default apache user
7    shell: sed -i 's/www-data/vagrant/' /etc/apache2/envvars
8    when: apacheuser_check > 0
9    notify: restart apache2
```

Puppet

```
1  exec { 'ApacheUserGroup':
2      command => "sed -i 's/www-data/vagrant/' /etc/apache2/envvars",
3      onlyif  => "grep -c 'www-data' /etc/apache2/envvars",
4      notify  => Service['apache2']
5  }
```

Chef

```
1  execute 'ApacheUserGroup' do
2      command "sed -i 's/www-data/vagrant/' /etc/apache2/envvars"
3      only_if "grep -c 'www-data' /etc/apache2/envvars",
4      notifies :restart, resources(:service => "apache2")
5  end
```

Ansible Sudo

We stripped the "sudo" from the snippets since usually it is defined in the playbook as default for all tasks.

Puppet Task Ordering

We avoided declaring dependencies since these are just quick reference guides, and the dependency requirement will depend on your own tasks flow.

Appendix One: Vagrant Changelog

This Appendix will list the new features coming with newer versions of Vagrant (starting with 1.5), so you can have a quick overview of what's new and where to find more information about it. Not all new features will be covered in this book, but the current content will be as up-to-date as possible.

Vagrant 1.6

Released May 06, 2014[50]

New Features:

- Global Status and Control
- New command: **version**
- Post-up Message
- Provisioner execution: once or always
- Windows Guests
- Built-in Docker Provider
- LZMA compression for boxes

Vagrant 1.5

Released March 10, 2014[51]

New Features:

---

[50]http://www.vagrantup.com/blog/vagrant-1-6.html
[51]http://www.vagrantup.com/blog/vagrant-1-5-and-vagrant-cloud.html

- Vagrant Cloud and Boxes 2.0
- Vagrant Share
- RSync Synced Folders
- SMB Synced Folders
- Hyper-V
- Improved plugin management
- Guest support for Funtoo, NetBSD and TinyCore Linux
- Password-based SSH authentication

Printed in Great Britain
by Amazon.co.uk, Ltd.,
Marston Gate.